Scholem, Arendt, Klemperer

Intimate Chronicles in Turbulent Times

Scholem, Arendt, Klemperer

Intimate Chronicles in *Turbulent Times*

Steven E. Aschheim

Published in association with
Hebrew Union College–Jewish
Institute of Religion, Cincinnati

Indiana University Press

BLOOMINGTON & INDIANAPOLIS

This book is based on the Gustave A. and Mamie W. Efroymson Memorial Lectures delivered at the Hebrew Union College–Jewish Institute of Religion in Cincinnati, Ohio, in October 1999.

This book is a publication of

Indiana University Press
601 North Morton Street
Bloomington, IN 47404-3797 USA

http://www.indiana.edu/~iupress

Telephone orders   800-842-6796
Fax orders   812-855-7931
Orders by e-mail   iuporder@indiana.edu

© 2001 by Steven E. Aschheim

The paper used in this publication meets the minimum requirements of American National Standard for Information Sciences—Permanence of Paper for Printed Library Materials, ANSI Z39.48-1984.

MANUFACTURED IN THE UNITED STATES OF AMERICA

Library of Congress Cataloging-in-Publication Data

Aschheim, Steven E., date
    Scholem, Arendt, Klemperer : intimate chronicles in turbulent times / Steven E. Aschheim.
        p.   cm.
    Includes bibliographical references and index.
    ISBN 0-253-33891-3 (cl : alk. paper) — ISBN 0-253-21446-7 (pa : alk. paper)
        1. Jews—Germany—History—20th century. 2. Jews—Germany—Intellectual life—20th century. 3. Jews—Germany—Identity. 4. Scholem, Gershom Gerhard, 1897– —Diaries. 5. Scholem, Gershom Gerhard, 1897– —Correspondence. 6. Arendt, Hannah—Correspondence. 7. Klemperer, Victor, 1881–1960—Diaries. 8. Germany—Ethnic relations.   I. Title.

DS135.G33 A7655 2001
920'.0092924043'0904—dc21
                                                                    00-061396

1 2 3 4 5   06 05 04 03 02 01

In memory of George L. Mosse—an extraordinary human being

Contents

Acknowledgments

This volume is based upon the Gustave A. and Mamie W. Efroymson Memorial Lectures delivered at the Hebrew Union College–Jewish Institute of Religion in Cincinnati, Ohio, between October 10 and October 14, 1999. It is a pleasure to record my gratitude to Michael A. Meyer for inviting me to give these lectures and for being such a gracious host when I was in Cincinnati. I must also thank Samuel Greengus and Stacia Deutsch of the Hebrew Union College who, with other members of the Faculty, showered me with kindness and hospitality. I would also like to place on record my gratitude to Janet Rabinowitch of Indiana University Press. From the beginning she expressed interest in this project, and she has supported it throughout. Melanie Richter-Bernburg proved to be an ideal editor—perceptive, considerably skilled, yet unobtrusive. I also want to express my appreciation of Batya Stein, who alerted me to the Wilde epigraph used in the introduction.

This book is dedicated to the memory of George Mosse. His caring wisdom, his delight in life and humanity, were an example and inspiration to all who knew him. The world has been diminished by his departure.

As always my wife, Hannah, and children have provided the loving foundations which alone make my work possible and worthwhile.

Scholem, Arendt, Klemperer

Intimate Chronicles

in

Turbulent Times

Introduction

This book draws its inspiration from some remarkable
documents penned by three extraordinary, and quite distinctive, German-Jewish thinkers: Gershom Scholem,
Hannah Arendt, and Victor Klemperer. These essentially
personal writings furnish us with chronicles that illuminate the formation, the deepening, and the transformation of their various evolving identities and worldviews as
they faced the great changes and cataclysms of the twentieth century. The texts in question have been published,
quite independently, over only the last few years. They
include the revelatory—adolescent and immediately post-
adolescent—diaries of Gershom Scholem, composed between 1913 and 1917,[1] and his mammoth lifelong correspondence, which he kept up until his death in 1982 (it
reads like a veritable "who's who" of modern letters); the
epistolary exchanges between Hannah Arendt and some
of the cultural luminaries of the century (Karl Jaspers,

Martin Heidegger, Mary McCarthy, Hermann Broch, and others); and the stunning chronicles of Victor Klemperer that trace in poignant, quotidian detail life in Germany from the 1880s on but which most dramatically document the dark period of the Third Reich.

Why put these texts together and with what justification? Klemperer, after all, was indelibly, and conspicuously, a creature of the Wilhelminian empire, steeped in its staid prejudices, preferences, and predilections. Born in 1881, a generational divide clearly separated his mental and political world, his patriotism and redemptive faith in the German spirit, from that of the more rebellious Scholem (born 1898) and Arendt (born 1906). While Arendt and Scholem were, indeed, Wilhelminian children, their sensibilities and sensitivities were associated with crisis and rupture: their formative moments revolved around World War I and the radical intellectualism of the Weimar Republic, respectively. It is this subversive, quintessentially Weimarian impulse that must account, at least in part, for their present resonance and Klemperer's doggedly old-fashioned Wilhelmianism, which renders him both extremely attractive and yet somehow attitudinally remote.[2] Yet, for Scholem and Arendt, too, it was ultimately their differences that seemed to be definitive. Their relationship was a stormy one that moved from admiration and friendship to overt hostility. (They also exchanged letters—some already published, the rest soon to appear in a separate volume.)

Indeed, all our protagonists were endowed with very different tempers and pursued apparently incompatible, perhaps even diametrically opposed, philosophical and political agendas. Their personal attitudes toward, and principled judgments about, the vexed issue of the relationship between *Deutschtum* and *Judentum*, Germanism and Judaism, had very little in common. Scholem, I am tempted to say, was a "primordial" Zionist, insistent upon the realization of a Jewish cultural and political renaissance in Palestine, intent on severing all German ties and influences; Arendt, on the other hand, though an idiosyncratically dedicated Jew and erstwhile Zionist, was suspicious of all collective and ideological labelings, far more provisional in her group commitments and conceptions of individual selfhood (a matter about which she and Scholem argued bitterly); and Victor Klemperer, a specialist in Romance languages and literature, distant cousin of the more famous conductor Otto Klemperer, was nothing less than a convert to Protestantism, a fervent advocate of *Deutschtum* and German-Jewish assimilation. Their ultimate geographical locations—Israel, the United States, and Germany, respectively—almost ideally reflected their diverse chosen identities and ideologies.

Again the question needs to be asked: Why put these testimonies together and with what justification? It is not sufficient to answer that these were all fascinating— albeit headstrong, opinionated, and at times infuriating— people (although they undoubtedly were). It is rather to claim that each of these texts adds compellingly to our knowledge of the world of modern German Jewry and that they do so from an unexpected angle: they are all personal documents revelatory of the most intimate aspects of the private self responding creatively to the vicissitudes of public experience. Taken collectively they yield a mosaic, a kind of composite portrait of the turbulent history of German Jews in the twentieth century—from Wilhelminian times, through World War I, the Weimar Republic, and the Nazi nightmare and its aftermath.

Moreover, despite the obvious differences between them, there *were* some important commonalities. Scholem, Arendt, and Klemperer were all highly articulate German-Jewish intellectuals, shrewd observers and analysts acutely sensitive to the pathologies and special contours of their times. They had in common an immense intellectual passion, a rare hunger for learning and understanding. Together with their contemporaries they responded to the great crises and historical transformations around them and sought to make sense of them; they, too, were confronted with problems, definitions, and options of identity ("German," "Jewish," "Zionist," "European," "cosmopolitan," and so on). Unlike many others who wrestled with these issues, however, they were able to provide sustained diagnoses, fresh answers, and alternative modes of understanding.

Though all were scholars with impressive publication records (and we shall certainly make reference to these), the emphasis here will be placed on their more intimate chronicles, their letters and diaries. Because, as a rule, these are less guarded documents, they tend to cast a more revealing light upon personal attitudes and intellectual processes than more formal, public utterances. One need not, of course, be quite as rhapsodic as was the young Gershom Scholem in his 1918–19 journal entries on the function of keeping a diary and the metaphysics of letter-writing, an activity which, in its purest form, he argued, could produce "the messianic moment":

> Among the greatest and most elevating phenomena is the liberation that a letter produces in one, like some absolute religion. The freedom of the letter is perhaps the highest freedom that writing which is not the Bible can achieve. At the beginning of every letter that deserves the name stands the *Schechinna* [the presence of God] and, imperceptibly, sings the most audible song. The writing of a letter serves the function of justice. . . . The perfect letter is signed out of meta-

physical necessity. To have a name is the deepest order of representation. . . . If the innermost essence of the world were not writing and language the letter would not exist. In letters individual being becomes scripture. . . . The diary has quite another function. The letter is religion, the diary also history, although there are real connections between them. But, a priori, the letter is not a diary.[3]

In our context, alas, these metaphysical musings must yield to the skepticism of the historian who, upon using such sources, should not approach them in quite as adulatory a fashion. Underlying the activities of keeping a journal and of sustained correspondence—with their mix of self-objectivating, self-discovering, and self-eliding potentialities—are to be found layers of complex psychological meanings and functions.[4] Letters can be artful and contrived. This was an explicit theme in the correspondence between Martin Heidegger and Karl Jaspers, both of whom played a crucial role in Hannah Arendt's intimate life and chronicles. "In letters what one has to say always comes out incompletely and 'written,'" Heidegger wrote to Jaspers, praising the greater expressiveness and honesty of the spoken word.[5] Diaries too, no doubt, can be compensatorily self-deceiving. Both are potentially self-serving forms—they may, consciously or otherwise, obscure or even repress, rather than clarify, the issues at hand.

Moreover, as Scholem suggests (though I think for different reasons), these are quite distinctive genres. Letters are by definition crafted for, and addressed to, a recipient; diaries are typically private. And yet, such distinctions are in practice too simplistic:[6] even if we do not perceive letters as vehicles of revelation (like Scholem—who left behind a staggering sixteen thousand of them!), they do very often provide glimpses into the inner world of the self that would otherwise be quite inaccessible; and certain diaries—Klemperer's is a classical example of this —receive their energy from and would be unrecognizable outside their inextricable connection with the public realm.[7]

Yet, all the necessary qualifications and distinctions notwithstanding, letters and diaries do have some important commonalities. Both are characterized by a unique immediacy. They provide privileged access precisely because of their peculiar temporal dimension: they inhabit the present moment in which the fluidity of affairs and the unfolding of the self is captured in process. Diaries— and also, to a great extent, letters—may dynamically reflect and capture, in ways that polished, post-facto reflective publications usually do not, "a state of turmoil or excitement, an inability to predict the future, an urge to master and purge overwhelming experiences or intense emotions."[8]

Certainly this is a description that applies to the letters and diaries of Scholem, Arendt, and Klemperer. More than any other materials they provide access to their innermost feelings and thoughts. Indeed, many of the letters and significant parts of the diaries examined here contain highly intimate material. At times, the reader may feel like an intruder, as if one were violating the writer's privacy. Yet, surely Wilde is psychologically very much on the mark. Like Cecily, our thinkers—each with a healthy ego and an acute historical consciousness— carefully left behind such documents in the knowledge (and probably the hope) that they might well, indeed, be published later.[9]

The historian is, of course, obliged to avoid voyeurism for its own sake and to employ these sources only insofar as they illuminate the substantive issues in question. Certainly it is not on such possible voyeuristic moments that the ultimate value of these documents rests. These intimate chronicles clearly rise above merely personal and passing matters. For they map and shed light on the turbulent times in which these thinkers lived and the very distinctive ways in which each conceived of, and coped with, the changes and challenges around them. They provide us with distinctive ideological maps, worldviews in the making, snapshots of options defined and pursued. They capture the respective conflicts, crystallizations, and articulations of identity. They lay bare the complex processes of reaction to, and interpretation of, problems and events as they occurred. They constitute a kind of illuminating "history from within," private records that reflect and somehow transcend the public realm and that register, from unexpected viewpoints, the thickness and drama of the twentieth-century European and Jewish experience.

1 Gershom Scholem | And the Creation of Jewish Self-Certitude

Gershom Scholem, we need hardly be reminded, was arguably *the* greatest scholar and thinker of matters Jewish in the twentieth century. It was through his easy mastery of vast fields of knowledge, his ability to present the esoteric byways of Jewish history in a thoroughly accessible, modern—indeed, radical—idiom that he excited so many readers whose worlds were entirely removed from that of Jewish mysticism. We are learning today, from a generation of his own pupils, that many of his particular insights in the field of Kabbalah—an academic discipline that he virtually invented—are in need of extensive revision. This will not, I believe, affect his stature as a great intellectual. Scholem created and was moved by a master vision. He possessed an intuitive grasp of, and profoundly identified with, the theological and metaphysical ground of things.[1] He constructed what we still admired in the days before postmodernism: a sweeping dialectical "philosophy of history," replete with an overarching theory of language; a conception of commentary as a vital force in the active shaping of a dynamic tradition; and a grand narrative plotting the structure, conflicts, and evolving meanings of Jewish existence—yet one steeped always in the minutiae of philological scholarship.

Scholem's works are by now relatively familiar—the secondary literature around his work is already extensive and impressive (Robert Alter's *Necessary Angels,* which originated within the forum of the Efroymson Lectures, stands out in this context).[2] In matters Judaic, moreover, I am not qualified to be either Scholem's expositor or his assessor. What I want to do here, rather, is to trace the construction of his distinctive person and the making of his (quite extraordinary) German-Jewish sensibility by documenting "from within," as it were, the ways in which he fashioned his self; rationalized his life-choices; and understood, and forcefully responded to, the formative events, issues, movements, and personalities of his times.

Scholem—like Arendt and Klemperer—was born into an acculturated family in 1898, during the period of the second German Empire. Although Scholem's Judaism and Zionism soon took on a highly idiosyncratic stamp, they are initially comprehensible only within the context of what Kurt Blumenfeld famously called "post-assimilationism."[3] Scholem belonged to a generation of culturally "assimilated" German Jews who were far removed from Jewish sources. Their Zionism combined an urgent awareness of their origins with a consciousness of the diminution, even the total lack, of their own Jewish substance and the passionate search for it. They rejected their elders' dominantly political and philanthropic form of Zionist identification and their rather unreflective faith in the easy compatibility of *Deutschtum* and *Judentum.* These younger nationalists formulated a more radical notion of Zionism as existential imperative, as personal transformation bound to the creation of an authentic cultural Jewish totality. They read, listened to, and were enraptured by Martin Buber's musings on Jewish primordiality and renewal.[4] They shared an explicitly "post-assimilationist" perception and impulse: while the psycho-cultural and ideational dimensions of their "German" identity were all too clear (and, in their view, problematic), it was the still rather inaccessible but nevertheless—what they took to be—primary Jewish self that had to be re-acquired, rediscovered. As Scholem's closest friend, Walter Benjamin, once put it: "I am learning Jewish [Ich lerne Jude] because I have finally grasped that I am one."[5]

The intensity of Scholem's commitments, the passion of his engagements, cannot be understood outside this generationally distinctive setting. For it was this context that allowed Scholem to exercise options not available only a decade or so earlier. But, of course, Scholem possessed genius. This exceptional man, the life and the work, cannot be reduced simplistically to the circumstances. The historian, disinclined to proffer speculative explanations or to indulge in dubious post-facto psychoanalysis, can only provide the relevant background. "To show a great individual shaping an identity, embedded in history and society yet drawing on the resources of a distinctive self," Michael Beddow correctly points out, "is an ambition biographers often profess but rarely achieve."[6] The question of the deeper forces that ultimately rendered Scholem the peculiarly powerful and original persona that he became lies outside the confines of this essay.

The recent publication of Scholem's youthful diaries[7] —begun at the ripe age of fifteen or sixteen—and his lifelong correspondence (including letters to and from his mother) does, however, provide us with a splendid moving picture of the unfolding of Scholem's inner world.[8] The diaries demonstrate a remarkably precocious, inquiring intellect, a highly charged eros channeled into a passionate mind. I say "channeled" advisedly, for these adolescent documents are almost entirely absent of reports of either sexual urges or romantic encounters.[9] Such omissions are even accompanied by an ideological gloss. In a wartime letter to Aharon Heller, reporting on what he describes as the horrible effects of sexual impurity on people (to which he had been privy in the German military), Scholem forcefully urged a kind of holy Jewish regenerative ascetism in sexual relations. "If we try to attain national health [*Volksgesundheit*] in the sense that the Germans are trying to become a healthy Volk, then we are lost, for here every access to the holy is blocked by obscenity."[10] Moreover, in keeping with the attitudes of these *Männerbund* times, the diaries are sprinkled with numerous negative allusions to women and their intellectual ineptitude.[11]

Scholem's chronicles do, however, reveal other kinds of fantasies—nationalist, religious, and messianic. His early mental world was not amorous but determinedly ideological and intellectual, even eschatological. The diaries refer to, and analyze, Goethe, Humboldt, Hölderlin, Rilke, Stefan George, Gustav Landauer, Karl Marx, Felix Mauthner, Kierkegaard, Jakob Böhme, and other, some more minor, masters. They demonstrate the not so surprising fact that this vehement critic of *Deutschtum* (Germanism) and assimilation was schooled in, and for his own subsequent work powerfully drew upon, the sources and categories of German classical, romantic, and avant-garde culture. They document the formative presence of, and the early admiration for, Martin Buber. But just as crucially, they also chronicle the emergent powerful critique of, and distancing from, that thinker. The diaries record the growing, disquietingly overdetermined distaste for Buber and his romantic-expressionistic cult of experience (*Erlebnis*), as well as the beginnings of Scholem's lifelong emphasis upon learning and direct, critical immersion in the sources. In connected fashion, they record the development of his famous friendship with Walter Benjamin.[12] (Because of the relatively familiar history of these relationships, I have chosen not to focus on them here.)

Scholem's journals contain remarkably mature meta-reflections on the relationship between freedom and history; musings on the philosophy of language (its task was to examine "language as the revelation of truth");[13] and ruminations that fused Scholem's emerging fascination with mysticism with his early immersion in mathematics: "Mysticism is . . . yes what is mysticism? Better, what is *not* mysticism? . . . Mystic is speech about the divine. Thus the plain paradox. It is not mysticism when one speaks to the One without the necessary awe. Mysticism is the experience (*Erlebnis*) of awe. There is no more abyss-like thing on earth than awe, and no one knows how to say anything meaningful about it. The mystic has sensed awe—who can conceive and represent this? The philosopher intuits something that is or will be, the mystic something that is not and will not be; he senses the simply impossible (only the mystic knows that God is *not*), he senses awe. The Holy. Mathematics is awe before thought. It is thus the crown of the human race: awe and thought, what can be more?"[14]

Many of the familiar shaping Scholemian categories, anarchist and Nietzschean, that gave form to his later analyses are already present in the adolescent writings: the fascination with transgression and danger ("Whoever desires to find himself must descend into the abyss and

seek himself in danger");[15] notions of paradox, dialectical
polarity, and antinomianism; the concern with the messianic; and the hidden connections between nihilism and
redemption.[16]

The young Scholem's travel diary of August 1914
with its reflections on mountain heights—on solitude, ecstasy, revelation—is stunning in its audacity. Indeed, it
reads like a religiously tinted gloss on Zarathustra.[17] There
is something strange and paradoxical here; for despite
Scholem's later, lifelong protestations of extreme distaste
for Nietzsche,[18] the philosopher is a formative figure in the
diaries, an inspirational crucible in the formation of his
radical and visionary sensibility (perhaps Scholem's protestations were one with his overall, esoteric predilection
for camouflaging his own intentions and persona).[19] Reading Zarathustra in 1915, Scholem waxed enthusiastic:
"Read *Zarathustra* again—one can absolutely and in no
way exhaust it. . . . one always finds sentences that surprise and strike one in one's own innermost being. . . .
One is constantly astounded by the power of its images
and the force of its language. . . . It is indubitably a holy
book, if one understands 'holy' correctly. Nietzsche has
of course declined the holy. And yet it is so. It is a holy
book because it speaks of man, because it speaks of the
overcoming of man, because it is a revolutionary book. I
love it."[20]

Indeed, in the young Scholem's mind, *Also sprach Zarathustra* became the living, inspired model for his own
path: "Whatever one may think of the ideas presented in
it, in fact this is a new Bible. Yes, it is written in such a
way that it is an ideal for me. This is it. To write a Jews'
Zarathustra (*Judenzarathustra*)."[21] Four years later and almost as tellingly, Scholem wrote in a letter to Aharon Heller: "I am sometimes beginning to believe that the only

person who, in these times, has said anything substantial about ethics is Friedrich Nietzsche."[22] Yet Scholem was already disingenuous about his immersion in Nietzsche. In the same letter he went on to tell Heller that of Nietzsche's works, "until now I admittedly knew *very* little and surely precisely the worst [Zarathustra]." This not only elided Scholem's various diaristic adulations of *Also sprach Zarathustra* but failed entirely, as he did in later years, to mention that as early as 1914 he *had* read a great deal of Nietzsche: the *Antichrist,* the various writings on Richard Wagner, and the *Untimely Meditations*—all of which he then compared unfavorably to Zarathustra.[23] Moreover, Scholem not only read many of the philosopher's works, he also devoured early on the famous Nietzsche-Overbeck correspondence which, as he emphasized in a letter to Werner Kraft, he had read in *one* night.[24]

We must return to Scholem's remarkable document of intoxication and revelation in the mountains, for it is here that the vision of serving his people unfolds. It is replete not only with Nietzschean tones[25] but also ringing religious and apocalyptic rhetoric. Thus spake the young Scholem: "Thy lonely child of man, why do you stand here. . . . will not the spirits and elements rise indignantly upon you, for you disturb and eavesdrop upon them in struggle? No, I will not weaken! For the storms' will brought me here. Now you are chaos, but eternal will brings forth renewal. Only in danger is God to be found."[26]

George Mosse has recently depicted Scholem, his life, person, and work, as an embodiment of the tradition of *Bildung* that characterized German Jewry's uniquely productive cultural and intellectual heritage and provided it with its peculiar humanizing face.[27] In this work I, too, want to argue that, for all their differences, it was this peculiar dedication to learning, the passion for knowledge and insight, that characterized Scholem, Arendt, and Klemperer. Still, Scholem's penchant for the demonic, his early and enduring intuition of what he called the "abyss," his fascination with the nihilistic impulse, his vehement critique of liberal-bourgeois rationalism, were, quite obviously, not a product of the quiet, ordering classicism of the German (or even Jewish) Enlightenment but cut directly from the cloth of fin-de-siècle "irrationalism" (and then spiced with a peculiar Jewish twist). "Reason," so reads one diary entry, "is a desire, but no reality. It is the longing of the dumb. . . . Everyone can be reasonable, but the Messiah is something special, he is unreasonable."[28] It was in the categories of *Lebensphilosophie* that the early Scholem shaped and channeled his idiosyncratic religio-nationalist affirmations. This went together with a sometimes violently formulated rejection of bourgeois rationalism. Thus he railed about his father and friends, atheists schooled in "science" and Haeckel's monism: "Beat them dead, this band of lice, deader, deadest, strangle them around the throat."[29]

Indeed, *Bildung*—that middle-class, gradualist, meliorist, inward doctrine of self-cultivation and bourgeois respectability—is attacked head-on. In Nietzschean tones of wrath Scholem declares in his diary: "To my People (*Volk*). It is the voice of a summons. Woe to those . . . that bring *Bildung* to their *Volk* and ruin and kill their brothers. . . . Woe to the *Volk* that seeks rebirth through *Bildung*. . . . For they rob my people of their creative powers. . . . No peace with the *Gebildeten*, saith my Lord. . . . You people and nations who want to remain healthy, keep far away from the palaces of culture. Your ways are not our ways and a holy war shall be kindled against you. For this is your death-illness, you from the House of Israel, that you have too much *Bildung* and adopted too many of the evil ways of your lands. Become what you were, that is, become natural, for that alone is your cure and salvation."[30] It was in this spirit that the early Scholem, addressing the *Jung-Juda* youth movement, still praised Buber, "because in Judaism, previously the classic religion of rationalism and logic-chopping, he discovered the irrational, emotion and yearning, which is the mother of renewal."[31]

If much of the later Scholem is already, more or less embryonically, present here, it is also clear that some parts of it should be regarded as expressions of adolescent *Sturm und Drang*. While the diaries, to a surprising extent, are indeed testament to the child as father to the man, I do not mean to suggest that nothing in the diary is exempt from the immature growing pains of youth, from developmental exaggerations. This applies especially and obviously to Scholem's by now famous youthful messianic vision as recorded in the diary on May 22, 1915: "Which of us young Jews, I wonder, has not had the same royal dream and seen himself as Jesus and Messiah of the downtrodden?"[32] It is noteworthy that this was formulated in relation to, though went pointedly beyond, the prophet of Jewish renewal, Martin Buber: "But he was not the redeemer. . . . He simply wanted to prepare the way for the masters after him; he sacrificed himself for these others, his blood-relatives [*Blutsgenossen*], whom he did not know. . . . He was not the redeemer."[33] If Buber was not the redeemer, then, clearly, Scholem was. (Scholem's vision paralleled other tendencies current in German culture at the time. Like almost all radical intellectuals of the day, he knew well the charismatic pretensions surrounding Stefan George and his circle.[34] Interestingly, his casting of Buber as the herald and himself—Scholem—as the fulfillment of the vision, replicated perfectly the way in which George was cast as the realization of the Nietz-schean dream.)[35]

The actual vision—from which we can here quote only sparingly—marvelously conjoins the prophetic with the learned, the world of knowledge with the messianic: "The young man goes alone through the world and looks around him, where the soul of his *Volk* awaits him. For he has a deep belief that the soul of Juda goes astray among the peoples and waits for him who would dare to free him from banishment and separation from the body of his people [*Volkskörper*]. And he knows in his depths that he is the one chosen to seek and find his people's soul. . . . The way of the innocent is the way of redemption. And the dreamer—whose name is already recognized as the awaited one: Scholem, the perfect one—prepares himself for his work and begins forcefully to forge the weapons of knowledge."[36]

This is fascinating because it gives us a highly intimate glimpse into the recesses of a young—and later famous—soul. Yet, one wonders, just how "intimate" it really was—or, at least, was supposed to remain. For much of this preciously and precociously self-conscious diary is written in this manifesto-like form, in the overtly declarative mode.[37] Be this as it may, it is clear that not all such moments should be treated with too much gravity. After all, less than three months after this vision Scholem himself recorded in his diary: "I do not believe any longer, as I did once, that I am the messiah."[38] Later in life, as Michael Brenner has pointed out,[39] Scholem became the leading student, rather than the practitioner, of messianism; but here, too, as in the rest of Scholem's life and work, the existential spark and the scholarly impulse were closely fused.[40]

Similarly, one should not overstate the importance of

Scholem's slightly later (August 1916) fantasy of creating a "society of zealots" (*Bund der Eiferer*) who would dedicate their lives purely and religiously to Zion.[41] This *Geheimbund* or secret society of the elect—a society like the "secret Germany" of the Stefan George circle—would have the task of acting as spiritual fertilizer for Jewish national renewal.[42] These juvenile fancies notwithstanding, the diaries nevertheless clearly demonstrate that Scholem's headstrong, and always powerfully reasoned, convictions about matters existential, Jewish, and Zionist were formed very early on and remained a constant part of his being. It was this certainty, the strength of conviction, that throughout his life made him such a central figure, always the relevant force against which the argument had to be made.[43]

Although, as we have already indicated, Scholem needs to be located within the contours of the "post-assimilationist" generation of German Zionism, even prior to his very early *aliyah* (emigration to Palestine) in 1923 through his death in 1982 there was nothing typical about him and his life. He was, in most respects, outstanding, exceptional—although, from our perspective, emblematic, representative of a certain choice, a path taken. The bare facts are well known (from the memoirs and other places): the commitment to a radical Zionism; the almost obsessive study of Judaism; the revolt against, and expulsion from, the bourgeois Jewish home; the distaste for, indeed, principled and conscious disengagement from, *Deutschtum;* the intuition that German Jews, in their passionate commitment to such a "Germanism," were simply living a lie.

As his rather *deutschnational* brother, Reinhold, pointed out in a letter in 1972: "Already in 1917 (perhaps even earlier) you removed yourself quite intentionally from a

German feeling. When in 1922 you 'naturally spoke Hebrew' you were already no longer a 'German Jew' but a
one hundred percent 'Israeli,' even though no such thing
existed then. Seen from this point of view, it seems to me
that your feelings and convictions did not coincide with
the majority of German Jews. You write that in the previous century the avant-garde elite left the German Jews
for *Deutschtum* and that the masses did not follow them.
Conversely you went into Jewishness (*Judentum*) or Is-
raeliness, but the Jews in their hoped-for masses did not
follow you."[44] Typically, Scholem did not take issue with
the notion, let alone the strange act, of conscious de-
Germanization; but in his reply to Reinhold, he indignantly noted that he had begun this process not in 1917
but at the "latest 1913. Naturally," he wrote, "I am in
no way characteristic of the majority of German Jews;
you are completely correct, and that is precisely the sad
point—that in their feelings and convictions the German
Jews were so fully deluded and, as a result of whatever
complicated spiritual processes, always self-deceiving."[45]

We will come back to the vexed and highly contested
issue of Scholem's harsh judgments concerning the comportment of his fellow German Jews; but certainly in his
case they cannot be dismissed as retrospective, as wisdom
acquired with the benefit of hindsight. In fact in almost
all matters of ideological and existential import the diaries
reveal a person who, from the age of fifteen or sixteen,
was guided by a kind of unerring inner radar. Scholem the
adult was by all accounts a formidable presence. That
same sharpness is already present here. One searches the
diary in vain for the expression of inner doubts of the
more conventional kind. Scholem was, to be sure, highly
rebellious; but his is a rebellion that proceeds as a kind
of inner unfolding, the powerful sculpting and refining

of that which is already there. In the very first entry—
Monday, February 17, 1913—he declares two commitments that were to remain with him throughout his life:
his contempt for *Galut* bourgeois Judaism—"I hate the
[liberal] Lindensstrasse [synagogue] where I was barmitz-
vahed"—and his almost instinctive affirmation of Zionism (at least as he idiosyncratically understood and constantly sought to deepen it).[46]

For him the putative conflict (or possible combina-
tions) between *Deutschtum* and *Judentum,* Germanness
and Jewishness, a relationship that preoccupied, often
in highly convoluted ways, many of the best (and also
the most mediocre) German-Jewish minds (we will later
see how Arendt and Klemperer dealt with similar questions), was from the outset a bogus issue. In 1917 he
wrote to his friend Werner Kraft: "The confrontation with
Deutschtum, which constitutes such a painful problem for
so many Jews, has never been that for me; and the fact
that I was raised in a totally non-Jewish environment did
nothing to change that. I have never sought nor found a
relationship with the values that first find their legitima-
tion in the German essence [*Wesen*]."[47] Scholem added
that this also applied to his relationship to the German
language, of which, ironically, he became one of the century's finest exponents. (Indeed, as early as November
1914, Scholem declares: "If I knew enough, I would write
this diary in Hebrew.")[48] Of Hermann Cohen's torturous
wartime harmonization of *Deutschtum und Judentum,* he
wrote simply, "an impossible text."[49] In a strange inversion of the usual order (non-Jewish antipathy for things
Jewish), Scholem had already openly pronounced his dis-
sociation from all things German while in school. Scholem's mother later recalled that one day at the beginning of 1915 the director of the school, Dr. Meyer, asked

Scholem's father to come to the school, where he was told that Gerhard (Scholem's pre-Hebraized name) had demanded that Germans and Jews be separated in the school. "We Jews and Germans," he exclaimed, "do not go together."[50]

Whatever the validity of Scholem's later thesis—that it was the Germans who consistently shunned dialogue with the Jews—in his own preemptive case, it was the Jew who denied any such intimacy.[51] When asked, in 1917, whether or not Fritz Heinle, Walter Benjamin's close friend who had recently committed suicide, was a Jew, Scholem responded in the affirmative and proceeded to embark upon a disquisition concerning the (im)possibility of authentic German-Jewish friendships: "I also believe that in fact such a relationship to a non-Jew would have been impossible. For the immanent distance between *Deutschtum* and *Judentum* is such and of such an essence, that perhaps here *everything* is possible, but only one thing not: a common life, in the serious sense. Only a miracle could bring it forth—a miracle that has not often happened, if ever—namely, a Jewish non-Jew."[52] (The miracle must have occurred, for Scholem was simply mistaken. Heinle was indeed a non-Jew.)

Jewish self-discovery in Germany, more often than not, was linked to some antisemitic incident, some form of rejection by the external environment. With Scholem this seems not only not to have been the case but also to have been more or less irrelevant. Instead, what Scholem intuited was the existence of a kind of primal Jewish substance—one that, in an environment foreign to it, was constantly being undermined and threatened. From the beginning Scholem thought not only in terms of essences but also in terms of a radical juxtaposition between such "German" and "Jewish" essences. The diary reveals an essentialist, explicitly *völkisch* Scholem. Thus he reports that his December 1915 meeting with Max Hodann of the *Frei-deutsche Jugend* (Free German Youth Movement) was particularly satisfying because the *völkisch* nature of both sides was openly and freely acknowledged: "He a German and me a Jew, and when I spoke the word Jew he made no painful face, but rather honored the other *Volkstum* just as I did his."[53]

For Scholem the marketplace of proposed fusions constituted something like a pollution of pristine realms. The "evil way" of the Jews, Scholem wrote to Gerda Goldberg, began when they ceased to want to be holy and confusedly came to accept "that a 'synthesis' between the determining orders of a foreign spirit and their own was possible."[54] This is how he put it in November 1916: "It is heretical . . . to hold as necessary a 'synthesis' of Judaism with 'West European' truths. . . . There is nothing from Western Europe that needs to be brought into Judaism. The spiritual orders should not be rendered impure [*verunreinigt werden*]."[55]

As early as October 1916, Scholem formulated a position to which, I believe, he adhered all his life: the nation, filled with religious content, was not a fleeting construction but an "essential determining force [*Wesensbestimmung*] of the inner form of Judaism. An *absolute* [emphasis his]."[56] Scholem, it is true, later adumbrated a conception in which Judaism contained an historical openness; but this openness operated within a given structure. Even when the tensions of this structure were highlighted, the process was by and large conceived organically, immanently.[57] Genuine change was change that occurred from within a "bedrock foundation" (where a transcendental truth was contained). The past dynamically evolved into the present but was always dialectically linked with its archaic origins.[58] Thus, modernizing movements that emanated from without—Reform would be one example—

produced only the degradation, or what he preferred to call the "liquidation," of Judaic substance. The vital forces challenging and reshaping, but necessarily responding to the imperatives of, tradition came always from the inside, even (perhaps especially) if they consisted of the most subversive, antinomian forces such as Sabbatai Zvi and the Frankists.

Whether or not Scholem, as Steven Wasserstrom has recently asserted, was implicated in the more general, "saving" project of a wider History of Religion, in which the esoteric, yet universal and transcendental, role of myths and symbols as such was central, even his most generally couched formulations were made within the parameters of an internally governed imperative.[59] It should be remembered that Scholem's association with the Eranos circle and such thinkers as Mircea Eliade and Henry Corbin, who were putatively associated with this project, began only in 1948, many years after all his basic ideas and intuitions had, so remarkably, crystallized. His post-Holocaust reflections on "Kabbalah and Myth" represented mature elaborations on organicist convictions formed much earlier:

> But if symbols spring from a reality that is pregnant with feeling and illumined by the colorless light of intuition, and if, as has been said, all *fulfilled* time is mythical, then surely we may say this: what greater opportunity has the Jewish people ever had than in the horror of defeat, in the struggle and victory of these last years, in its utopian withdrawal into its own history, to fulfill its encounter with its own genius, its true and "perfect nature"?[60]

Neither the young nor the later Scholem, then, had difficulties—as our own post-modernist generation does —speaking in the language of separate, demarcated Jewish and other "essences." "Germanness" and "Jewishness" were, quite simply, conceived as radically opposed substances. The problem with Hermann Cohen's utopian, fictional attempt to create an identification between, a harmonization of, *Deutschtum* and *Judentum,* he wrote later to Karl Löwith, was that it entailed whitewashing and destroying both essences.[61]

This was clearly an autobiographically grounded ideological blindspot; for when Scholem—himself so obviously a product of the culture he so disdained—vehemently insisted that men like Kafka, Benjamin, and Freud (incidentally, Scholem's second wife, Fanja, was part of the Freud family) considered themselves to be only Jews and in no way thought of themselves as Germans, he was not only indulging in a form of simplistic essentialism foreign to these thinkers themselves but also refusing to recognize a core component of the German-Jewish intellectual adventure. There were moments when Scholem did grant a greater complexity to these issues. Thus, though he would never himself have emphasized this dimension, he did not dissent from the assertion of his friend George Lichtheim that Freud necessarily had to stand outside his Judaism in order to accomplish his scientific work.[62] (Scholem conducted both an ongoing, exciting intellectual exchange and a touchingly caring, personal correspondence with Lichtheim, famous as a scholar of Marxism but less known as the translator into English of Scholem's *Major Trends of Jewish Mysticism.*)[63] In general, however, he was unwilling, or perhaps unable, to see that such admixtures, the necessary and unanticipated forms of hybridity, were the motor of as much intellectual productivity and cultural inspiration (in these as well as other thinkers) as it was of confusion and, occasionally, distress. Indeed, this upsetting of simple dichotomies constituted a vital ingredient and achievement of the German-Jewish experience.

Moreover, part of the later admiration for Scholem

(in contradistinction to Buber and many other German-Jewish luminaries of the time) was his principled opposition to the Great War and his refusal to engage in the prevalent mass war enthusiasm. But the diaries make abundantly clear that his posture derived not so much from a sense of outraged humanism but—in far greater measure—from the belief that the worlds of European and German politics were simply not a Jewish-Zionist matter. In January 1915 he wrote of his friends "that they so misunderstand Zionism if they think that on the slaughterfields of Europe in a sea of blood and murder renewal and resolution for Juda occurs. Our way is revolution, and it does not proceed from the corpses of west European strangers. What is assimilation if not this? You are all halves, and my great fear is that if Herzl were alive he would be on your side."[64] A little later—in "A Lay Sermon," an article he wrote for his own youth journal, *Die Blau-Weisse Brille* (September–October 1915)—he went even further, protesting the way in which the struggle for Zion was being mixed with this mass murder: "Will it go on? Will the way to Zion still proceed through the main cities of Europe? . . . We want to draw a dividing line between Europe and the Jews. 'My thoughts are not your thoughts and my ways not your ways.' We have not sufficient people to throw them voluntarily to the wrath of Moloch. No we need people who . . . are close to their own people. . . . For we want to be drunk and intoxicated with our own *Volk.*"[65] Scholem generalized this sense of civilizational conflict even more widely when, in 1930, he wrote to Edith Rosenzweig: "I am convinced that the time is coming when a confrontation, in a catastrophic sense, between Judaism and Christianity will become necessary. . . . "[66] (For all these rejections, it should be noted that Scholem was throughout aware of the paradox—involved in his early move to Palestine—"that I, a complete and untransformed enemy of Europe [*Europafeind*] and follower of the new Orient, who wants to be the bearer of a new Juda, must be content with making the move precisely as the teacher of European knowledge [*Wissenschaft*].")[67]

The nature and source of the Jewish spiritual order, this distinctive substance, was not problematic for Scholem as it was for so many of his and previous generations. Of the Bible, he noted in January 1916: "I think that for us Jews still today, the Bible is something inborn, part of our innate tribal inheritance, about which perhaps one does not know anything; but once it enters into consciousness, from that hour the person affected knows that this is a Holy book and that this has nothing to do with God."[68]

Scholem's inner compass never seems to have wavered. What emerges so clearly from these early incidents and opinions—even if we concede that part of the overflow, the excess, can be accounted for in developmental, adolescent terms—is a certain kind of fanaticism. Scholem, often self-ironically,[69] approved of the description. In 1916 he noted in his diary: "They 'know' me now as an intolerant fanatic—thank God!"[70] One of the first entries (in March 1913) declares: "I relate everything I see to Judaism and contemplate it as such. Perhaps one can regard such a standpoint as one-sided. But that's the way I am."[71] In November 1914 he proclaimed: "We are the coming ones, everything is in our hands. We have chosen and make no compromises."[72] This feel for, the insistence upon, totality, was a highly self-conscious one. "Everything I wish for myself," he confided in his 1916 diary, "that I would want to write on my gravestone, I could summarize epigrammatically without lying: *He was his name.* He was Scholem [*shalem*], that is whole, he was as his name demanded, he lived his name, wholly and undivided."[73] Perhaps, given the "assimilationist" times in which he lived and the "outrageous" program he set for himself, such single-mindedness may have been necessary (as perhaps it was also in his brother Werner, who turned to Marxism and Social Democracy as part of *his* alternative rebellion. The debates between the two brothers over the merits of their rival ideologies, of organization and anarchism, their observations on the philosophy of history and dialectical materialism, Scholem's early, sharp critique of Marxism—a lifelong opposition—constitute one of the small joys of this correspondence).[74]

This forcefulness (never entirely absent in Scholem's adult incarnation either) was pervasive and applied in equal measure to his insights into, and rejection of, *Deutschtum;* his assessment of German Jews; his passion for philosophical, Judaic, and mathematical study; his revolutionary brand of Zionism; his radical commitment to self-discovery (and self-transformation) through re-Judaization, the total immersion in Hebrew and his belief in its redemptive, purificatory qualities. Jews, Scholem indignantly informed Siegfried Lehmann, could not "grasp the living word of God in the German language, only from the innermost center of the Hebraic soul can the inner form of Judaism be comprehended."[75] "I am learning Hebrew," he informed his diary in 1916, "as I will learn no other language. Judaization grows proportionally to growing close to Hebrew; but at a certain place, one is suddenly sprung into the center of the language, and one's soul is revealed."[76] Hebrew, he noted to himself, was the instrument of radical self-transformation, learned properly only when one could be silent in it.[77]

It is the force and totality, the radicalism of his convictions that constantly strikes the reader. Who else but Scholem could have written such a diary entry: "What I have now . . . come to see with irrevocable clarity, truth and distinctness, is that I do not fit in with these people here, these German Jews. I cannot meet one of these people, be it man or woman, without something—[their appearance] or an unconscious agitational streak of mine —driving me to be honest, totally honest, with them; and I have seen that, without exception, a heaven-wide abyss separates me from these people. . . . one sees immediately they know nothing of greatness, have seen nothing of the unbourgeois nature of things [*Unbürgerlichkeit der Sache*]."[78] The words he wrote many years later (1963) about Carl Gustav Jung could just as easily have applied to himself: "Greatness has an effect like an intrusion of the transcendental and is a task of life that borders on the extreme."[79]

The impassioned turn to Zionism represented just such an extreme, a radical personal and collective turn, the antidote to bourgeois shallowness. As he noted in November 1916: "I am occupying myself always and at all times with Zion: in my work and my thoughts and my walks and also, when I dream. . . . All in all, I find myself in an advanced state of Zionization, a Zionization of the innermost kind. I measure everything by Zion."[80] Even earlier, on the second anniversary of the outbreak of the Great War (August 14, 1916), Scholem breathtakingly exclaimed: "the goal and meaning of life is called: Zion."[81]

Scholem defined this early Zionism within his own idiosyncratic and critical terms—his often contemptuous criticism of his fellow believers is well known. Here was a vision animated by anarchic, experimental, indeed, revolutionary (though spiritual rather than conventionally political) impulses. His diary entry in January 1915—

bursting with rebellious élan—dismissed Herzl as "formalistic," *State*-oriented. "This," he exclaimed, "we reject. For we preach anarchism. That is: we want no State, but a free society (with which Herzl's *Altneuland* had little to do)."[82] Achad-Ha'amian and Marxist versions of Zionism were similarly rejected as vestiges of an evolutionary, rather than revolutionary, conception. Although Scholem was later to reject (in characteristically vehement form) much of Buber's teachings[83] (was Scholem possible without Buber?), this was a Zionism that emerged from Buber's notion of an inner and outer "renewal of Judaism." But Scholem articulated this revolutionary impulse with rare passion and heat, even enchantment and ecstasy.

One of his earliest published letters, of August 29, 1915, declares: "Spiritual movement is not evolutionary, like the slowly swelling flame of holy light; no, it is a leap, is shattering and revolution—the awakening race (*Geschlecht*). It does not move in a line, especially not a straight [one], but in hyperbolic, that is, inconstant, ramified curves (forgive a mathematician these mathematical images); spiritual movement is explosive . . . whoever has experienced it knows that where there is something new, something unheard of, there spirit is to be found. . . . Also, what is essential about Zionism is only that which becomes new, vital only is the creative synthesis."[84] In its Scholemian incarnation, Zionism was rupture and rapture, an essentially revolutionary, especially antibourgeois, creation, one that, as he put it in his diary, proceeded "above the depths and through the undiscovered, the unexplained."[85] (Years later, in conversation with George Mosse, he reiterated that given the radical precariousness of Israeli existence, the Zionist project could not possibly be bourgeois; for was not security the very essence of bourgeois life? There were no guarantees in what amounted to a kind of Pascalian historical wager.) We must now get back our bearings. Scholem's path —like that of Arendt and Klemperer—traversed the great historical events and moral dilemmas that affected especially German Jews in the twentieth century. It revolved around choices concerning the life of the mind; the nature of interpersonal relationships; Jewishness; taking a stance on the connections (or lack thereof) between *Deutschtum* and *Judentum* and on Zionism; and, of course, confronting National Socialism. Scholem's answers to the questions, controversial as they may have been, were clear. His very early departure for Palestine in 1923 left little room for doubt. (Arendt left Germany when—and because—the National Socialists came to power in 1933; Klemperer, as we know, spent his entire life in that country and died in 1960 in the German Democratic Republic.)

Scholem's magisterial scholarship aside, his very early dismissal, his unswerving proclamations on the impossibility, of the German-Jewish dialogue, accompanied by the act of *aliyah,* has given him a certain moral stature, the reputation of something of a clairvoyant. Of the eventual fate of German and European Jewry at the hands of the Nazis, George Steiner has recently written that Scholem was possessed of a virtually unique (though "helpless") "clear-sightedness" and was amongst the very few who sounded a "warning."[86] To be sure, Scholem's Zionist narrative rendered him sensitive to currents hostile to Jews. But we must be exceedingly cautious here: there is nothing in the record that even approximates a prediction, or warning, of what was to come. There are references in the diaries and early letters to the writings of some antisemites, but these are occasional, not systematic. Surprisingly, nowhere—neither in the earlier nor in the later postwar period—does he provide a considered historical analysis of the development and particularities of German antisemitism.[87] Even more pointedly, despite his obvious and intense interest in these events, Scholem never attempted (either in published form or private correspondence) a sustained concrete treatment of the specificities of the nature, rise, and disposition of National Socialism, or of its atrocities and their overall place within German history. It was above all Hannah Arendt—as we shall see—who, albeit very controversially and problematically, confronted the novum head-on and sought to work through its distinctive moral, political, and cultural implications, to forge new tools of thinking, novel categories of analysis appropriate to an unprecedented eruption. (Victor Klemperer in his own way also did this, but his insights were derived from the realities of everyday personal experience and not based upon reflections arrived at from a more comfortable distance.)

There may be many reasons for this analytic absence in Scholem. In the first place, he was hardly alone. Few people—until well into the 1960s—were able to absorb, let alone comprehend, the radically transgressive, taboo-defying character of post-1941 exterminatory Nazism. Indeed, to this day we have trouble constructing a coherent narrative and are still haunted by the apparent lack of theoretical and cognitive tools necessary for apprehending this unprecedented reality.[88] In any case, more than any other available option, the conventional Zionist version offered something like a coherent, familiar frame, a recognizable, comprehensible narrative in which antisemitism was placed at the center.[89] There was also geographical and temporal distance (something that certainly did not apply to either Arendt, at the beginning, or Klemperer).

Referring to the persecution of Austrian Jews after the *Anschluss*, Scholem wrote to Walter Benjamin that such events took on a more or less "abstract" character: "it's just too far away, and nobody has any real notion of what it might be like."[90] Indeed, most tellingly in the intimate letters between Scholem and his mother, Betty, there is virtually no discussion at all until 1939 of the need to leave Germany; and when, eventually, the matter arises, it is raised not by Scholem but by his mother.[91] Early on Scholem writes that though Palestine will always provide a possible refuge, it is essentially a place for the young and that other possible destinations should be sought. This attitude is, perhaps, explicable in everyday human terms. Perhaps, like many other children, one didn't want one's mother too close. Yet there is nothing even vaguely prophetic in his April 1933 assurance that one needed courage, and that even the worst of circumstances could change.[92] And, soon after, Scholem advises that "one must take it philosophically. Perhaps times would come again that the German *Volk* would know and comprehend that the Jews were not so horribly dangerous."[93] (One does not want to make too fine a point of it—it is only because of his supposed prescience that this is pertinent—but as late as March 1936 we find Scholem giving his mother exceedingly detailed instructions on luxuries she should bring from Germany on her impending trip to Palestine: "If you want to bring me something special, apart from chocolate marzipan, there are many possibilities: for example, six really good shirts with attached soft collars, size 41, but really good quality, grey-blue and cream colored. Or material for a *very good* blue suit. Or in case you think that all of this is not affordable, 2 good dark red ties without any pattern.")[94]

This does not at all mean that Scholem was not

alarmed by, and concerned with, these events. Early on he was aware of the historical magnitude of developments[95] —but this was a generalized perception, not limited to critics of Jewish assimilation. Indeed, it was the highly assimilated Victor Klemperer who wrote in December 1930: "No one knows what will happen but everyone feels the coming of a catastrophe."[96] Scholem's pronouncements seldom revolved around a differentiated analysis of German society or the nature of the regime itself. Both before, during, and after the Nazi period they were almost always motivated by and centered upon a criticism of the mind-set and behavior of the German-*Jewish* middle classes within German society (a critique which, as we have seen, was formulated long before the onset of Nazism).

At some level, no doubt, Scholem's work on messianism—conceived essentially as a theory of catastrophe— and his reading of Lurianic Kabbalah as a negotiated Jewish recovery in the light of the Jewish expulsion from Spain, is related to the great traumas of his time. It may even be, as Steven Wasserstrom has recently suggested, that in their radically new critical analyses, both Freud's classic *Moses and Monotheism* and Scholem's pioneering and inspired essay on Sabbatai Zvi and Jacob Frank, "Redemption through Sin" (both were published in 1937), represented a paradoxical response to the Nazi assault: "Freud dethrones a prophet king, and Scholem, so to speak, glorifies a Jewish scoundrel. In both cases, this paradoxical strategy was explicitly undertaken by Jewish writers during the Third Reich as a paradoxical kind of national self-defence. . . . Audacity withstood catastrophe by means of a preposterous moral inversion of historical reasoning."[97]

The thesis (as well as the comparison) is intriguing, yet, in our context, not quite satisfactory. This is not only because it does not sufficiently take into account Scholem's lifelong penchant for radical and transgressive paradox (a predilection that both predated and postdated the Nazi period and that animated his Zionism and writings on religion and Jewish mysticism throughout). It is rather to argue that while Scholem's *Jewish* writings were often deliciously coded—"one must," he proclaimed, "learn to read books against their declared intentions"— his proclamations on Nazis and Germans were always remarkably direct. The subversive notion of "redemption through sin," of evil being fought with evil, appears in his work and thought as an internal doctrine, one that occurred dialectically within Judaism, not as a political prescription of how Zionism was to recreate itself and combat National Socialist terror.

For Scholem, the model for what was happening was clearly not Sabbatai Zvi but rather, explicitly, the traumatic expulsion from Spain. But even in this case, he wrote, there was a crucial moral difference between Hitler's Germany and Spain. In the latter there were no (assimilated) "national-Spanish" Jews, and Jews thus had more of their own substance. "We have learned much about Jewish history over the last two months," he wrote in May 1933, "a lesson that [will] hopefully one day bear fruit."[98] "Will things remain as they are, or will they give way to even bloodier conditions?" Scholem wrote to Walter Benjamin from Palestine in April 1933. "The horrible thing about it, though, if one dares to say so, is that the human cause of the Jews in Germany would only stand to benefit if a real pogrom were to take place, instead of the 'cold' pogrom that they will be trying to restrict themselves to. It represents almost the only chance of bringing about something positive from such an eruption. For, although the extent of the catastrophe is of his-

toric proportions, and it can teach us something about
1492, the stuff of which resistance is made has been reduced in German Jewry to a very small fraction of what
existed in those days. The magnitude of the collapse of the
communist and socialist movements is frightfully obvious,
but that of German Jewry certainly does not pale by comparison."[99] For Scholem, the problem with assimilation
was that it was not only morally dubious, it inherently
also distorted judgment and weakened action.

But while his interest and concern in these matters
was clearly intense, he did not undertake anything ap-
proaching his own interpretation of Nazism. All that we
have is stated in the form of critique. Thus he devastat-
ingly and accurately criticized Horkheimer's "Europe and
the Jews," which reduced antisemitism and Fascism to the
dynamics of capitalism, as a prostitution of dialectics;[100]
and he famously upbraided Hannah Arendt (his friend of
earlier years) for what he took to be the unfeeling arro-
gance of her *Eichmann in Jerusalem.*[101] Indeed, even earlier,
in January 1946, he took her to task for her depiction of
Zionist involvement in transfer politics with the Nazis as
a form of Jewish betrayal.[102]

Of course, all later discussion on this topic bears
the imprint of Scholem's famous insistence upon the self-
deluding, undignified nature of the "German-Jewish sym-
biosis." But his stance, it is important to note, was always
more a moral critique of *Jewish* comportment, a Zionist
indictment of craven assimilation—ethical, not political in
character—and certainly not a concrete, nuanced analysis
of the perpetrators and the catastrophe.[103] Indeed, as we
have seen from the diaries and the early letters, and as
Scholem himself later conceded, he came to this conviction *years before* the Nazis came to power.[104] German Jewry
had lived a "lie," Scholem told Karl Löwith in August

1968, one which eventually had to resolve itself one way or the other (this in itself is a fascinating but highly contestable proposition). But, he explicitly emphasized, such a lie in no way necessarily had to lead to extermination, to the *Judenmord*—"*none of us thought that*" (was keiner von uns gedacht hat).[105]

But if "the lie" that German Jewry lived was not connected to the "Final Solution," Scholem never really tells us what were the relevant connections. He thus leaves the explanatory gap wide open and nowhere, as far as I have been able to make out, attempts to fill it. He does not furnish an analysis of the historical phenomenon of Nazism, of its rise to power, or its horrific brand of racism or, for that matter, of the murderous dynamics of the "Final Solution."

When it came to the realities of the hell to come then, Scholem was no more clear-sighted than others; and the "warnings" to which Steiner refers were really indignant admonitions of the self-abnegating comportment of his fellow German Jews, not prescient visions of their victimizers' future plans and actions. But it is also important to highlight Scholem's denial that there was no connection between craven German-Jewish assimilation and their later tragic fate. This is important because a great deal of the subsequent historiography of German Jewry and Nazism has been framed within—and contested around—Scholem's terms of reference. Scholem's most formidable adversary in this respect has been Peter Gay, although annoyingly he seldom, if ever, mentions Scholem by name, a fact that outraged Scholem. As Scholem told Robert Alter —whose review of Gay's *Freud, Jews and Other Germans* he admired[106]—"It is a book written in full knowledge of my stand in these matters and against me. You say quite rightly that he [Gay] makes no reference to my name in the whole book, but he quotes verbally from my essay 'On Jews and Germans' without naming me. . . . He says that this is exactly the position against which he will write. I envy your tact and generosity which I would have been unable to mobilize in writing about this rather scandalous book. The title is really a perfect Chuzpa. Freud all his life considered himself a Jew and nothing else. If I have any occasion . . . I shall surely quote Peter Gay as a classical example showing to which length glorifiers of Jewish assimilation to Germany are prepared to go 35 years after Auschwitz."[107]

Gay's strongest statement reads thus: "Why were Germany's Jews so blind, so self-deluded? Did they really believe they were Germans or was this so-called conviction only a pure convenience, an intellectual laziness, if one does not want to characterise it even more sharply as high treason? These are not neutral questions based upon purely historical interest. They consist of an attack, an accusation. These questions all too often have taken on an ugly form. . . . What Hitler did to the Jews—so goes the reproach—they deserved. It was a gruesome but not totally unjustified punishment the Nazis meted out to the assimilated Jews that had betrayed Judaism. The Nazis as agents of an incensed Jewish God—it sounds bizarre, rather inhuman, but precisely this reproach lies hidden in these hostile questions and is often expressed. And this reproach is . . . one that German Jews have had to live with for decades."[108]

Whatever position one adopts on this vexed issue, Scholem and Gay, it would be wise to note, replicate and perpetuate at the level of historiography older historical conflicts that pertained to the polemics between German-Jewish liberals (assimilationists?!) and German Zionists. The mutual recriminations are exaggerated, lack proportion. Thus Scholem's comments, quoted above, on the need for a "pogrom," shocking though they may be, were designed specifically to alert German Jewry to a reality that, Scholem believed, they could be made to see and that could thus *save* them from their future fate. There is no hint here or in his later comments of an obscene belief that—given their obsequious behavior—they "got what they deserved." At the same time, Scholem's simplistic dismissal of Gay's position as "chutzpa," as a mere glorification of what he unproblematically labels "assimilation," does not even begin to confront the complexities of the "mixed signals" German Jews had to negotiate and interpret, nor their exciting and productive adventure with modern culture, their creative appropriation of non-Jewish materials for purposes of Jewish redefinition and renewal, or their dilemmas and multifarious responses. Any post-Nazi historiographical assessment of that experience is duty-bound to examine these dimensions with the seriousness they demand (and as far as possible—how much is indeed possible?—without the benefit of hindsight).

But, in our context, that surely is the point. Scholem's insights concerning Germans and Jews were always penetrating and forceful, sometimes hugely illuminating, but —here I will apply a phrase I heard once while listening to Saul Bellow—those more of the bird than the ornithologist. His contempt for assimilation, his belief in separate German and Jewish essences, his insistence that dialogue (however defined) was a mere delusion must be regarded less as dispassionate analysis of a complex historical reality than as an expression—indeed a projection—of his own powerfully articulated convictions, his moral outlook, the cultural and political directions taken early on in the course of his own life and history. They register the assumptions and possibilities—the grandness and vi-

sion as well as some of the blind spots—of one extraordinary German Jew as he confronted the great questions
and events of his time, one who made certain clear-cut
choices while forging a formidable sense of Jewish self.

It is time now to turn to two other quite remarkable, equally emblematic, German-Jewish thinkers whose
choices and moral and political outlook were quite different, indeed, radically opposed and yet, whose sensibilities
may have been far more similar than any of them would
have suspected, or indeed, appreciated.

2
Hannah
Arendt

And the

Complexities of

Jewish Selfhood

We sorely need, I think, a history of German-Jewish and non-Jewish friendships, of marriages and intimate relations, their successes and failures. This would provide a necessary corrective to the view of all German-Jewish history, in the light of its terrible conclusion, as a history of unremitting hostility and estrangement. Very often, it is true, what appeared on the surface as real friendship ended in recrimination and hostility. Ritchie Robertson has recently written that such relationships were based upon a perceived inequality of power that was characterized by a sycophantic, fawning—and usually unfulfillable—desire of the Jew to be respected by the more powerful, norm-setting Gentile.[1] This, certainly, holds in numerous cases. It captures, as he reminds us, the relation of the Jewish philosopher, Theodor Lessing, to the notorious antisemite Ludwig Klages (Lessing was himself a complex example of the psychological convolutions he analyzed in his most famous work, *Jewish Self-Hatred* [1930]).[2] But it rather flattens the more complex dynamics—the attractions and hostilities, the mutual dependencies and fears, the proud self-consciousness on both sides —that pertained, say, to the fascinating relationship between Freud and Jung.[3]

In need of serious examination is Gershom Scholem's assertion (as a young man) that real friendship, authentic intimacy, could not really occur between German Jew and non-Jew. Certainly this cannot be affirmed in an either/or manner; the realities here are multiple. For instance, if we take the case of Walter Benjamin (a close friend of both Scholem and Arendt—and yet another source of friction between them), this highly sophisticated theorist was, indeed, uncritically admiring of (the far cruder) Bertolt Brecht, who in turn was often curtly dismissive of him. Yet, Benjamin's friendship with Fritz Heinle, who committed suicide during World War I, was so deep that Scholem was convinced that Heinle was a Jew (which he was not).[4] Moreover, as we shall see in the next chapter, no marriage could have yielded greater fidelity and trust under conditions of unremitting terror than that between the (converted) Jew Victor Klemperer and his (Protestant) wife, Eva.[5]

Hannah Arendt (1906–75) was an iconoclastic intellectual, political theorist, philosopher, historian, Jewish activist, Zionist (of sorts), and author of diverse works ranging from her early biography of Rahel Varnhagen to her master work on *The Origins of Totalitarianism* to the infamous *Eichmann in Jerusalem* (with its denial of antisemitism as the driving force behind bureaucratic mass murder and its indictments of the Jewish Councils as agents of Nazi destruction) to more philosophical tomes such as *The Human Condition* and *The Life of the Mind* (to name just a few). She provides us with an ideal example of the richness, ambiguities, limits, and complex possibilities of such intimate relations. Her prodigious published correspondence raises in peculiarly acute form issues pertaining to the vexed connection between the personal and the political realms. It graphically demonstrates the concerns that shaped the direction and nature of her creative work and the making of her original German-Jewish persona. Her exchanges of letters with Kurt Blumenfeld[6] (a leader of German Zionism), tellingly entitled "Rooted in no possessions" (". . . in keinem Besitz verwurzelt"), and with Hermann Broch,[7] that great, unjustly neglected Austrian Jewish novelist (author of the masterpiece, *The Death of Virgil*), are compelling.

But most revelatory is the sustained correspondence with non-Jews who played crucial roles—personally and intellectually—in her life. One such obvious example is that of her friend Mary McCarthy.[8] It was, however, with non-Jewish German men that the passions and influences were really played out, the issues illuminated. (Perhaps Scholem's dictum concerning the impossibilities of intimacy was made in the spirit of the German *Männerbund* tradition and thus meant to apply only to relationships between men.) The respective correspondence with her lover and teacher from the Weimar years, the philosopher Martin Heidegger[9] (the highly controversial relationship is reflected in an exchange of letters spanning fifty years); with her lifelong mentor and friend Karl Jaspers;[10] and with her second husband, Heinrich Blücher,[11] render very questionable the claim that such German-Jewish relationships and intimacies were virtual impossibilities. Indeed, they exemplify precisely the kind of dialogues Scholem claimed never existed: dialogues in which Jewishness often played an explicit, even a defining, role. This, then, may be yet another reason why the Scholem-Arendt relationship, built as it was upon both deep commonalities and severe differences, was so fiery, illustrative of the most basic questions at issue among German Jews. The Scholem-Arendt letters, too, will demand our attention.[12]

We have here an embarrassment of riches. Each of these sets of correspondence merits sustained exposition and reveals different dimensions of a complex personality confronting vexed issues. Arendt, no doubt, was almost instinctively combative and sometimes very nasty. Who else could have written—as she did to Hermann Broch— that "these Hungarian Jews à la [Arthur] Koestler did not become any more pleasant, even if one denies Hitler the right to kill them"[13]?

But Arendt also had a lasting penchant for personal loyalty and friendship. These were humanizing values which, characteristically, she integrated into the body of her thought. Friendship (rather than brotherhood), a free and lively exchange of opinions, incessant discourse about the world and its affairs—not absolute and dogmatic truth —were her central values.[14] These gave her reflections on Gotthold Ephraim Lessing—himself famous and favored among German Jews for his paradigmatic friendship with Moses Mendelssohn—a peculiarly personal and experiential quality. (In retrospect one wonders to what extent in this text Arendt's decisive opting for the values of friendship and humanity over truth should also be read as a kind of gloss on her relationship with Heidegger.)[15]

Certainly in the realm of friendship Arendt achieved something quite astonishing. Taken together, the erotic love letters with Heidegger and Heinrich Blücher, and the heartfelt confessions of friendship and kinship between her and Karl Jaspers, must surely be regarded as high points in the intimate lyrical literature of the German language in the twentieth century. A singular quality of Arendt's person must have elicited this. It is no coincidence that all these admirers drew attention to Arendt's almost radiant fusion of the sensual and the cerebral, her physical and spiritual sides.[16]

We must begin with the—already much analyzed—question of the Heidegger-Arendt link, rendered especially controversial given the later, ineluctable association of Heidegger with National Socialism, his notorious subsequent refusal to seriously engage the Shoah, and Arendt's continued association with him (to this day critics bitterly berate her for the "attack" on the Jews in her Eichmann book as she blithely continued her friendship with and defended someone as indelibly tainted by Nazism as was Heidegger). Here I will concentrate only on those matters pertinent to our present concerns—the quality and nature of the relationship, the issue of Jewishness, and the connections to Arendt's creative and intellectual worlds.

In many ways this was indeed an asymmetrical, unequal relationship. It began in 1925 at the University of Marburg when Arendt, an impressionable, bright-eyed nineteen-year-old student, first met Heidegger, seventeen years her senior and the revered, rising star in the world of German (and later, world) philosophy. That Arendt was overawed should come as no surprise. Very soon, the liaison went beyond the bounds of intellectual passion, and one of the great academic love affairs of the century got under way. (It must be stressed that, however stormy the physical side of the affair may have been, it was relatively short-lived.) It is not difficult to imagine Arendt's responses to the advances and letters of the charismatic philosophical revolutionary of the time. And we do have to imagine this since the early letters are overwhelmingly

Heidegger's. Arendt was far more likely to have kept his letters than the dissimulating, married Heidegger was to have kept hers—assuming they were written at all. This may be taken as another index of the unequal weight of things.

Our intention here is not to document in torrid, gossip form, as did Elzbieta Ettinger,[17] the detailed instructions Heidegger gave as to when Arendt was to make her illicit nocturnal visits (certain lights in certain rooms had to be turned on or off), at which places on the railway routes to meet, or when to destroy the notes that had been written. From a distance they read as a peculiar mix of passion, philosophico-amorous purity and, to some degree, patronizing exploitation. Nevertheless, it was Arendt who, in a desperate gesture to assert some kind of independence, broke off the affair and in 1929 entered into a short-lived marriage to Günther Stern, though the early ecstasy remained: "Do not forget me and do not forget," she wrote to the philosopher that year, "how much and deeply I know that our love has become the blessing of my life. That knowledge cannot be shattered."[18] The truth of that statement was soon verified, Arendt's vulnerability rendered palpable, by the immense shock, pain, and insult when, soon after, Heidegger snubbed her.[19] There was little question as to who was the dominating party. Pointedly, almost the only sustained words from Arendt in the early correspondence is called "Shadows" and is revelatory not only of her sexual and intellectual ripening but, as the title indicates, also her subservience, surrender, malaise.[20] In this correspondence there is virtually no serious philosophical exchange, no discussion of ideas between equal intellectual partners.

The ties between Arendt and Heidegger continued convulsively through Arendt's death in 1975 by way of a series of breaks and epiphanic reconciliations. The breaks were prompted above all by the jealousies and antagonisms of Elfride, Heidegger's viciously antisemitic wife. Elfride, Arendt wrote to Blücher, had made Heidegger's life "hell on earth": "The woman, I fear, will be prepared to drown all Jews as long as I live. She is, unfortunately, simply murderous."[21] Yet, this obstacle apart, and despite the reconciliations, the asymmetry of the earlier days persisted: Arendt continued to admire Heidegger's genius while he remained insultingly indifferent to her work. Arendt was acutely aware of this ongoing dynamic, and her exasperation occasionally found expression. She put it thus to Gertrud and Karl Jaspers in 1961: "I know that he finds it intolerable that I appear in public, that I write books etc. All my life I've pulled the wool over his eyes, so to speak, acted as if none of that existed and as if I could not count to three and sometimes even to four. Then I suddenly felt that deception was becoming too boring, and so I got a rap on the nose."[22]

For all that, it seems, Arendt was never able to really transcend this first passionate love, especially with a man whose genius, as she wrote to him in her letters as late as the 1970s, had "created real room for thought"[23] and who "read as no one before" had read.[24] It should not, then, come as too great a surprise that—by means of the problematic strategy of splitting Heidegger's philosophical from his political side—a much-criticized Arendt undertook the postwar task of rehabilitating this "secret king of thought," writing laudatory articles, and initiating and supervising English translations of his works.

These, then, are the raw narrative biographical materials. How can they be interpreted in the light of our concerns? In the first place, if a certain lack of reciprocity is to be detected, this by no means constitutes the whole story. While it is true that the bourgeois conventions had to be strictly observed—had the married Heidegger been discovered he would have been dismissed from his position —and while there were indeed exploitative moments, Heidegger's passion, his deep feeling for Arendt, seems to have been genuine enough (even if, initially, it derived in part from the thrill of the forbidden). It certainly was remarkably articulate. From the beginning through the end of their relationship, Heidegger wrote Arendt radiant love poetry and letters (even if there are moments when the Heideggerian style may strike one as cloying). "I have been touched by the demonic," he writes early on. "Nothing like this has happened to me before."²⁵ "Nothing," he wrote after an evening spent together, "stands between you and me. The most simple being together—without restlessness and demand, without questions and deliberations—so entirely tranquil that I would have shouted with joy, had not the awe of this moment made me even more blissful."²⁶ Indeed, in April 1925 Heidegger explicitly and lovingly tells Arendt that she has energized, directly inspired his work and thought: "I should no longer say 'that, you do not understand.' You, you sense it—and come along. There are 'shadows' only where there is *sun*. And that is the ground of your soul. Right out of the middle of your existence you are near to me and have become always an influential force in my life."²⁷ This was an affair, as George Steiner puts it, that unleashed "great powers of concentration and creation. . . . The period of *eros*, of sexual mastery coincides with the genesis of *Sein und Zeit* [Being and Time]."²⁸

These passions and never broken ties notwithstanding, it is necessary to place the relationship in proper perspective. In the first place, one must note the very obvious: the love affair took place many years before the Nazis came to power. Moreover, if Arendt was later never entirely able to release herself from the magician's spell (woven by a thinker who, no matter how problematic his story may have been, continues to be regarded as one of the two great philosophers of the century), she was aware not only of the characterological weaknesses of the man (even if too often her emphasis on that side of Heidegger elided some of his actions as a consciously "conniving opportunist")[29] but also of his ideological biases. The recurring hints and accusations that Arendt's entire project was infected by the continuing influence of, and loyalty to, a man deeply complicit in Nazism holds very little water. Indeed, I think that it can be demonstrated that while Arendt's thought-world is indeed unthinkable outside the Heideggerian universe, she radically transformed and in so doing rather thoroughly negated it. The great watershed, the experiential filter, was of course Nazism; and in her private communications, as well as in her public pronouncements (such as the 1947 "What Is Existential Philosophy?"),[30] Arendt's judgment can hardly be called clouded. Of Heidegger's conduct, she wrote to Blücher in 1950 that it consisted of the "same mix of authenticity and mendacity or better cowardice—both ultimately derive from the same source."[31] There is a marvelous fable of the—only apparently sly—philosopher's convolutions and ultimately self-defeating machinations in her 1953 *Denktagebuch;* it is called "Heidegger the Fox," and the concluding lesson reads: "Nobody knows the nature of traps better than one who sits in a trap his whole life long."[32] After numerous meetings with him during this period, she declared: "With Martin actually . . . there is nothing 'terrible,' only sad. Nothing has changed and nothing will."[33]

Heidegger's "silence" about the Holocaust has become

notorious.[34] Arendt, however, attempted to force him to engage the problem in various private conversations. When given no choice but to confront the issue, the philosopher typically resorted to a tactic that Arendt immediately identified: "In the last few days," she wrote in April 1952, "I got nothing more out of him. He constantly tried the same [tack]: through endless comparisons and rational elucidations he relativized all particular events, for instance, now also the gas chambers. . . . It is all really just a game."[35] (This was the same line Heidegger adopted with Herbert Marcuse in their correspondence, where he equated the extermination of six million Jews with Allied treatment of East Germans, and Auschwitz with motorized agriculture.[36] Many years later—in the mid-1980s—this tactic would become even more scandalous when Heidegger's student, Ernst Nolte, published variations of these arguments in what was to become known as the *Historikerstreit*.)[37]

Heidegger was talking, one should not forget, to the author of *The Origins of Totalitarianism*, which had already appeared in 1951. This was perhaps the first serious work to try to come to grips with the radical, transgressive nature of Nazism and which sought to provide a narrative commensurate with the gravity of the event. Of course, Arendt's emphasis on "totalitarianism" was also comparative—Hitler's Germany and Stalinist communism were the archetypal cases—but the burden of her analysis was clearly to demonstrate the radical nature of Nazi evils, not to relativize and excuse them.[38] For Arendt—quite unlike Heidegger—*this*, specifically, rather than an entirely undifferentiated technological modernity, was the great caesura. Upon learning of Auschwitz in 1943, she later reported: "It was really as if an abyss had opened. . . . This ought not to have happened. And I don't mean just the number of victims. I mean the method, the fabrication of corpses and so on. . . . Something happened there to which we cannot reconcile ourselves. None of us ever can."[39] In one way or another, she spent the rest of her life seeking to comprehend the making of this genocidal mentality and to understand its implications. As she put it to Kurt Blumenfeld while composing the book in 1947: "You see I cannot get over the extermination factories."[40] From the beginning she was convinced that only new forms of thinking could grasp this great transgressive moment in European history. As one contemporary of hers, Alfred Kazin, put it, "the life of the mind was of no use unless addressed to the gas"; and it was precisely this that Arendt did.[41] (That quest, as we shall see, was graphically evident in the probing, experimental correspondence Arendt conducted with Karl Jaspers.)

This is not the place to rehearse her analysis—I have done so elsewhere in great detail.[42] Here we must limit ourselves to the ways in which Heidegger is reputed to have been linked to her understandings of Nazism and the Shoah. Very conspicuous—and to some extent problematic—is the fact that Arendt entirely omits factors of German history and continuity from her account. There is absolutely no hint in her narrative of the *Sonderweg,* of the weight of political and social developments peculiar to Germany. Similarly, all connections to the role of tradition, indeed culture itself, are utterly dismissed. As early as 1945 she declared that the Western, and especially the German, tradition, "Luther or Kant or Hegel or Nietzsche[,] . . . have not the least responsibility for what is happening in the extermination camps."[43] Nazism was about the breakdown, not the realization, of tradition and culture; its sources were to be found in nihilistic rupture, not continuity.

Ernst Gellner has interpreted Arendt's unwillingness
to look at direct German influences, to indict cultural pre-
dispositions and popular attitudes rooted in that society,
as a "strange refusal," explicable in terms of the fact that
Arendt herself was raised in, and remained wedded to,
those same suspect intellectual traditions that were appropriated by Nazism—especially as incarnated in romanticism and by Heidegger.[44] Richard Wolin has even argued
that Arendt's exculpation of mind and culture from responsibility for Nazism is a function of her reconciliation
in 1950 with her ex-lover Heidegger, whom she regarded
as the veritable embodiment of this culture.[45] But this is
conceptually and chronologically distorted: Arendt had
already made this analysis of Nazism and its uniqueness
in the 1940s, when the connection to Heidegger was entirely severed. And her "strange refusal" to examine con-
tinuities may have had less to do with the Heidegger connection than with the (still persuasive) conviction that
Nazism was a radically new phenomenon and as such required new conceptual equipment adequate to the ana-
lytical task.

It was precisely because Arendt regarded totalitarianism as going beyond all previous limits, rendering "everything possible," that she saw its roots not in terms of continuity but rather in terms of breakdown. It is true that
she located these processes of disintegration in the rise of
a leveling "mass society," very much a conservative "Weimar" idea and one that was also adumbrated by Heidegger. But the latter would never have dreamed of specifically applying it to an analysis of Nazism and the Gulags.
For Heidegger, the death camps required no special attention, they were simply absorbed into the generalized, undifferentiated phenomenon of mass technological modernity. Arendt went in search of the specific roots of such

barbarism and discovered them in the processes of uprooting and atomization, spearheaded by a novel and radical bourgeois politics and economics of expansion for its own sake in which everything—the nation-state, tradition, culture, indeed people—becomes superfluous. Surplus capital produces the precondition for genocide: surplus people. *The Origins of Totalitarianism* thus both married and transformed the influence of Arendt's two great loves: it idiosyncratically fused the Heideggerian conservative theory of mass society with a radical (and insufficiently remarked) Marxist analysis of imperialism, much of it borrowed from her communist husband, Heinrich Blücher.

It is true that Arendt's disinterest in constitutional liberal democracy,[46] her analysis of the horrors of mass society in general,[47] the emphasis on thinking without metaphysical props and her overall working categories (especially as formulated in *The Human Condition*) are inconceivable outside the Heideggerian universe. Yet, even more importantly, her biography—especially the acute consciousness of her Jewishness, her refugee experience at the hands of Nazism, and her horror at Auschwitz—induced her ultimately to create a philosophico-ethical universe that was not only opposed to but indeed provided a stark alternative to the Heideggerian world. This cannot be elaborated on here; suffice it to say that whereas Heidegger disdained the political and had only contempt for the meaningless "chatter" of the public realm, Arendt furnishes the twentieth century's most radical affirmation of the autonomy of the political in which—in contrast to the monolith of the totalitarian experience—human plurality stands as the central public fact and value. Moreover, while Heidegger built his thought upon Being-toward-Death (and after the *Kehre*, upon passively opening oneself to "Being"), Arendt became the first philosopher to make birth, natality, the ability to begin ever anew, the cornerstone of her thought.[48] (There is an irony here. Arendt remained childless. So too did Scholem[49] and Klemperer. This is surprising in such productive, vital people. Perhaps their eros was ultimately exclusively deflected into intellectual realms. As surprising as the fact of childlessness itself, however, is the remarkable, almost total, absence of reference to this condition in their letters and diaries.)[50]

Arendt's emphases upon, and affirmations of, the autonomy of politics, plurality, and natality obviously cannot be divorced from the Jewish and totalitarian experiences of the century. We are back, therefore, to the question of Jewishness and the Arendt-Heidegger relationship. Here a definite limit was reached. As we shall see, with Jaspers Arendt discussed Jewish affairs unapologetically and in depth; with Blücher the discussion proceeded in a wholly relaxed, uninhibited manner. With Heidegger, the topic had a kind of brooding presence—lurking in the background, it was mainly avoided or evaded. When it was raised, the tone was strained, even confrontational (as in Heidegger's winter 1932/33 reply to Arendt's queries concerning a rumor about his antisemitism)[51] or simply obfuscatory, as in Heidegger's strictures that "Being" required a different mode from that of ordinary thinking, a different form of memory in which the "destiny of Jews and Germans would acquire its own truth," unavailable to conventional historical reasoning.[52] Indeed, given the circumstances, when in 1950 Arendt renewed the relationship, there was something plaintively disingenuous in her insistence to the philosopher that: "I have never felt myself to be a German woman and for a long time have ceased to feel as a Jewish woman. I feel . . . like a girl from nowhere (*Mädchen aus der Fremde*)."[53]

Arendt's decision to finish her dissertation under Karl Jaspers in Heidelberg must have been both a source of relief and resentment to Heidegger. The relations between these two leading men of letters turned out to be exceedingly complex and jagged;[54] and ironically, it was, in the end, Arendt, the German-Jewish woman, who provided the only mediating connection between them. As Heidegger told Arendt: "The *real* 'and' between 'Jaspers and Heidegger' is only you."[55]

Arendt's move to study under Jaspers began a lifelong, remarkable friendship.[56] It was a friendship that, among other things, made it possible for her to gain a different, more critical, perspective on Heidegger. To be sure, the matter is complicated, for both Jaspers (rather uncomfortably) and Arendt were convinced that Heidegger's foundational philosophical acumen remained in a class of its own.[57] Nevertheless, their dialogue did help Arendt articulate her own far more affirmative conception of politics, plurality, and the public realm. In 1946 it was already clear that she favored Jaspers's declared aim: not to produce results but to "illuminate existence" through "communication[,] . . . the preeminent form of philosophical participation."[58] Heidegger, on the other hand, she argued, was characterized by a philosophical "solitude" leading inexorably to a (National Socialist form of) "nature-oriented superstition": "Heidegger has drawn on mythologizing and muddled concepts like 'folk' and 'earth' in an effort to supply his isolated Selves with a shared, common ground to stand on. But it is obvious that concepts of that kind can only lead us out of philosophy and into some kind of nature-oriented superstition. If it does not belong to the concept of man that he inhabits the earth together with others of his kind, then all that remains for him is a mechanical reconciliation by which the atomized Selves are provided with a common ground that is essentially alien to their nature. All that can result from this is the organization of these Selves intent only on themselves into an Over-self in order somehow to effect a transition from resolutely accepted guilt to action."[59]

This analysis clearly linked Heidegger's *thought* (rather than merely his character) to his Nazi turn. Moreover, in implicit contradistinction to the example of Jaspers, Arendt objected to Heidegger's predilection for claiming the removed status of privileged knowledge for philosophy —especially his own.[60] Thus, in 1957, while acknowledging his genius, she declared to Kurt Blumenfeld that Heidegger "cites himself and interprets himself as if it is a text out of the Bible. I simply cannot tolerate it any more."[61]

Jaspers had married Gertrud Meyer, the daughter of a devout Orthodox Jewish family, in 1911. They survived the Third Reich precariously as a "privileged mixed marriage" (the Klemperers were, as we shall see, a "simple" mixed marriage). Early on Jaspers and his wife determined upon a mutual suicide pact in the event of arrest. (Like the Klemperers, their bonds of intimacy held even under the most brutal pressures.) Two weeks before their planned evacuation—on April 14, 1945—Heidelberg was liberated by the Americans. Of course, Jaspers's bravery and untarnished record under Nazism, coupled with his pioneering 1946 *Die Schuldfrage*,[62] the first postwar document to attempt to come to grips with the criminal, political, and ethical dimensions of German guilt, made it much easier for Arendt to discuss with him, openly and critically, Jewish and other sensitive matters in a way that was unthinkable with Heidegger.[63] But even before the rise of National Socialism, this candidness characterized their exchanges. Like a sequence of intellectual snapshots, the correspondence traces their engagement with, and changing attitudes to, questions of Germanness and Jewishness and, later, the nature and consequences of Nazism. Theirs was what Scholem would perforce have deemed an authentic German-Jewish dialogue. For it was on the *basis* of Arendt's and Jaspers's—admittedly idiosyncratically conceived—commitments to Germanness and Jewishness that their relationship took on so much of its energy and significance. It should be quite clear—especially in light of her later critique of Zionist politics, the Eichmann book, and the great rift with both the Jewish communal establishments and Scholem—that Arendt never in the least hid either her Jewish or Zionist commitments.[64] Indeed, both before and after World War II she made these programmatically central and explicit, especially to her non-Jewish friends. "Politically," she declared to Jaspers in 1946, "I will always speak in the name of the Jews."[65] Of course, the Shoah sharpened her articulation of this point. She put it thus in her 1959 Lessing address: "In the case of a friendship between a German and a Jew under the conditions of the Third Reich it would scarcely have been a sign of humanness for the friends to have said: Are we not both human beings? . . . In keeping with a humanness that had not lost the solid ground of reality, a humanness in the midst of the reality of persecution, they would have had to say to each other: A German and a Jew, and friends."[66] Her 1964 prescription for German-Jewish relations was formulated even more strikingly: "there should be a basis for communication precisely in the abyss of Auschwitz."[67]

The Arendt-Jaspers correspondence contains fascinating discussions and differences in interpretation about being a "German" and a "Jew." Their January 1933 dialogue concerning *Deutschtum*, the nature of Germanness, acutely mirrored the troubled times: Arendt's sensitivity

to the rumblings of antisemitism and Jaspers's (still tradi-
tionally conservative and nationalist) naïveté as to the
brutal nature of the developments beginning to unfold
around him. Jaspers—with Max Weber as his model—
had spoken in terms of German "essences" and "national
character." Arendt took exception to his notion as "something absolute, something untouched by history . . . I cannot identify with that, because I do not have in myself . . .
an attestation of 'German character.'"[68]

But it was not merely on the abstract question of essences that Arendt differed with Jaspers. The real sticking
point was the place of the Jew in German society. Arendt's
reservations were couched in terms of a Weimar Zionist
sensibility she had appropriated from her mentor of the
time, Kurt Blumenfeld. When it came to questions of Germany's political destiny, "I as a Jew can say neither yes
nor no. . . . For me, Germany means my mother tongue,
philosophy and literature. I can and must stand by all that.
But I am obliged to keep my [political] distance." Language and culture were one thing—historical and political destiny another: "I know only too well how late and
fragmentary the Jews' participation in that destiny has
been, how much by chance they entered into what was
then a foreign history."[69]

If the young Arendt saw matters very much through
Zionist-colored spectacles, she was already adamant about
refusing the validity of pre-cooked ideological recipes, for
she hastened to add: "What my Germany is can hardly be
expressed in one phrase, for any over-simplification—
whether it is that of the Zionists, the assimilationists or
the anti-Semites—only serves to obscure the true problem
of the situation." Jaspers's response was deeply touching—if rather uncomprehending. "How tricky this business with the German character is! I find it odd that you

as a Jew want to set yourself apart as a German." The whole point, Jaspers insisted, was to provide *Deutschtum* with ethical content. "That attempt," he wrote—his words endowed with an aura of nobility given that they were written in 1933—"however would have proved successful only if you, too, could say: That's the way it is. I want to be a Geman."[70] Jaspers, it should be noted, maintained this position throughout. "What it comes to in the end," he declared in 1952, "is that I will never cease claiming you as a 'German.'"[71] (This rarefied conception of *Deutschtum,* as we shall see, coincided very much with what Victor Klemperer so ardently—but in vain—sought amongst his contemporaries.)

The Arendt-Jaspers exchanges about Jewishness were equally frank and revealing. Between 1929 and 1933 Arendt was working on her study of Rahel Varnhagen (which was eventually published, in English, in 1957).[72] That work, about the famous Berlin salon Jewish woman who lived from 1771–1833, her inner conflicted Jewish world, and her attempts to assimilate, was conceived against the backdrop of increasing antisemitism during the Weimar Republic and was animated by a peculiarly German brand of Zionist critique: it contained many of Arendt's seminal, sometimes dazzling, insights into the tortured duplicities and psychology of assimilation—the notion that in the modern era Judaism was transformed from an objective way of life, an impersonal system of belief, into "Jewishness," a psychological quality, a personal problem—that were incorporated into her later work.[73]

Jaspers objected passionately to the way in which Arendt had portrayed Rahel. The details of the debate, which was conducted in the fashionable existentialist discourse of the day, lie outside the limits of this discussion; however, Jaspers later summed up its ongoing emo-

tional and symbolic stakes this way: "I wanted to defend
. . . the many remarkable people who have lived as German Jews."[74] He took exception to Arendt's ideological
stance, her implicit Zionist standpoint ("One does not es-
cape Jewishness"), her critique of Enlightenment assumptions and, ironically enough (given the enmity that later
developed between them), a very Scholem-like argument
against the possibility of an authentic German-Jewish
dialogue. "Rahel seems to have wakened neither your interest nor your love," Jaspers chastised his student. "The
book takes Rahel as a point of departure to then deal with
something altogether different." Rahel had to be seen "not
just in the context of the Jewish question, but, rather in
keeping with Rahel's own intentions and reality, as a human being in whose life the Jewish problem played a very
large role but by no means the only one. . . . Rahel was a
human being, liberated by the Enlightenment, who trav-
elled individual paths that didn't work out for her and that
ended in blind alleys, but she also remained on the one
true way, and that persists despite her failure."[75]

Ironically, many of the reprimands Arendt directed
later at Scholem replicated Jaspers's critical comments
about her own dogmatic, ideological line. But time did
modify her position. By 1952, while she continued to
maintain that for Rahel the Enlightenment had indeed
"played a highly questionable role" and that her own Zionist critique of assimilation was still valid (though she
found it necessary to add that it "was as politically naive
as what it was criticizing"), she did make some new, crucial distinctions in the light of the Nazi experience. "I am
afraid," she wrote, "that people of goodwill will see a connection which does not in fact exist, between these things
and the eradication of the Jews. All this was capable of
fostering social hatred of the Jews and did foster it, just as

it fostered, on the other side, a specifically German breed of Zionism. The truly totalitarian phenomenon—and genuine political anti-Semitism before it—had hardly anything to do with all this."[76]

We have already mentioned Arendt's conviction that the analysis of National Socialism required entirely new categories and modes of analysis. The correspondence is replete with the process by which such ideas took shape, the give and take, the forming of a picture adequate to the enormity of the events in question (an exchange that continued through the book on Eichmann and beyond). The pages resonate with passionate discussions and disagreements as to how to conceive of National Socialism, its crimes and guilt. For Arendt these exploded "the limits of the law; and that is precisely what constitutes their monstrousness . . . we are simply not equipped to deal . . . with a guilt that is beyond crime. . . . This is the abyss that opened up before us."[77] Jaspers, on the other hand, warned that "a guilt that goes beyond all criminal guilt inevitably takes on a streak of . . . satanic greatness— which is, for me, as inappropriate for the Nazis as all the talk about the 'demonic' element in Hitler. . . . we have to see these things in their total banality. . . . Bacteria can cause epidemics that wipe out nations, but they remain merely bacteria. I regard any hint of myth and legend with horror, and everything unspecific is just such a hint. . . . The way you do express it, you've almost taken the path of poetry."[78]

We cannot here pursue Arendt's fascinating answer.[79] What is relevant in the present context is the fact that only the highest degree of trust and intimacy facilitated this sense of open exchange and reciprocal criticism. (Of course, in public their stances were mutually defensive and laudatory.[80] Jaspers was well aware of his student's

combative instincts, and as she prepared for the Eichmann trial he presciently—and protectively—warned: "I
am afraid it cannot go well. I fear your criticism and think
you will keep as much of it as possible to yourself.")[81] Both
recognized that a crucial part of their selves lay in this
consciously German-Jewish friendship. As Arendt had
written elsewhere, only where there was continual discourse about the affairs of men could there be friendship;
and where friendship reigned, so too did humanness.[82]
This was a friendship that matched a passion for public
affairs with the deepest personal trust.

Here, indeed, was a German-Jewish dialogue. But
it clearly took place among free-thinking intellectuals
who represented no establishment or accepted communal postures. Indeed, both Jaspers and Arendt explicitly
challenged what they took to be the unreflexive, self-
celebratory nature of group affiliations. It is precisely the
complexity of Arendt's commitments and self-definition
that makes it so difficult to simply label her. On the
one hand, her Jewishness and interest in matters Jewish
(though not Judaic) were never in question; indeed, they
were at times even strident. "I belong [to the Jews]," she
wrote to Scholem, "beyond dispute or agreement."[83] But
unlike Scholem it was not an absolute identification. It
was most clear under conditions of persecution, as she
put it, where one resisted "only in terms of the identity
that is under attack."[84] And if, as she told Jaspers, politically she spoke "only in the name of the Jews," she immediately qualified this by adding, "whenever circumstances force me to give my nationality."[85] Ultimately she
resisted all totalizing definitions, insisting that no single
or homogenizing identity and identification adequately accounted for the disclosive complexities of selfhood (emphases that became integrated into the performative focus

of her work at almost every level). When asked by Jaspers whether she was a German or a Jew, she replied: "To be perfectly honest, it doesn't matter to me in the least on the personal and individual level."[86] This problem of group versus individual loyalties was, as we shall see, very much part of her conflict with the Zionists and the Jewish establishment. Arendt clearly relished the complex, even subversive nature of her own intertwined commitments. Thus her second husband, Heinrich Blücher, was not only a non-Jew, he was of working-class origins and so nonconformist a German Marxist that as an adolescent he joined the Zionist Blau-Weiss group.[87] She thus summed up her view to Jaspers: "If I had wanted to become respectable I would either have had to give up my interest in Jewish affairs or not marry a non-Jewish man, either option equally inhuman and in a sense crazy."[88]

With Blücher the mix of these identities mingled most comfortably, the intimacy was easiest, reinforced by the fact that both met as fugitives from Nazism in France. At the very beginning of their acquaintance in 1936, Arendt told Blücher that, unlike her best friend (Rahel Varnhagen), whose Jewishness drove her all the time to justify herself, one should never do so.[89] Their affinity applied equally to matters intellectual and amorous. The early love letters are remarkably erotic and moving, deeply intimate.[90] Thus, Heinrich's letter of February 21, 1937, freely translated, says: "I can no longer distinguish if all the light that I can discover in this great world is directed at you and then defines and transfigures me, or even more, that all the light that radiates out of you and warms me helps to illuminate the beautiful things of this great world for me. . . . You, mine, do you still know that I am the man whose lot it is to sound out thy depths—who has the anchor in which to anchor you—who has the earth borer to release all the living sources of passion from you —who has the plough in which to plough you thus, that all the energizing juices become alive in you? You Hannah, do you not also long for me, as I long for my sea, my haven, my sources, my own earth?"[91]

The small moments—Arendt's pride when Blücher beats Walter Benjamin in a game of chess—are memorably touching.[92] Moreover, her letters to her second husband—inconceivable with either Heidegger or the more patrician Jaspers—are freely peppered with Jewish expressions (*nebbich, meshpoche,* and so on).[93] Very soon after meeting Blücher she dubs him "my beloved wonder-rabbi," boasts that she is the only German Jewish woman who has ever learned Yiddish[94] and, reporting to him about a 1936 meeting of the World Jewish Congress—the proceedings of which were partly conducted in Hebrew— comments that "after all my dismal attempts to learn it, is no language, but a national misfortune! So, my love, don't let yourself be circumcised."[95]

The varied nature of Arendt's individual relationships and intellectual commitments brings us closer to the nub. They reflect the reality of, and begin to explain, the complexities of Arendt's Jewish selfhood. For we should not forget that—beginning with her critiques of political Zionism[96] and climaxing with the highly controversial *Eichmann in Jerusalem* in 1963—Jewish communal establishments (and many identified Jewish intellectuals) relegated her, for all intents and purposes, to the status of an adversary, an "enemy" tainted by "self-hating," even antisemitic, impulses and condemned her as a thinker whose tone and work had violated the most cherished taboos of group solidarity and propriety. What made Arendt so annoying, so difficult to pin down, was precisely her *involvement,* the fact that her life and thought were passionately linked to core predicaments of the Jewish experience. It was her partial "insider" status, her troubling—but always idiosyncratic and sometimes subversive—engagement and relevance that rendered her so threatening. She is best understood in terms of Michael Walzer's portrait of "connected critics,"[97] those figures whose life and thought are characterized not by detachment but by passionate, yet essentially ambiguous, engagement. This rendered not only her challenges but also the responses to them particularly charged, emotionally overdetermined.

It is here—both in terms of their personal relationship and the differing emphases of their work—that a comparison with Gershom Scholem is in order. At first their Jewish and Zionist commitments seemed to dovetail easily. Indeed, in 1941 Scholem described Arendt as "a wonderful woman and an extraordinary Zionist."[98] What ultimately and profoundly divided them, what underlay the rift, was the issue of group loyalties and solidarity. We have already analyzed the sense of total, albeit highly sophisticated, commitment that characterized Scholem's project; Arendt viewed matters differently. This was expressed in her famous response to Scholem's 1963 admonition that she lacked *Ahavat Israel*. "Love," Arendt insisted, was not a collective, national emotion: "I indeed love 'only' my friends and the only kind of love I know of and believe in is the love of persons."[99] For Arendt, loyalties were multiple and cross-ethnic. In 1955 (well before the Eichmann trial) she wrote to Blumenfeld concerning Scholem: "I cannot tolerate this nationalist chatter that isn't really seriously intended and that springs from a quite understandable anxiety. And this gossip about the goyim gets pretty much on my nerves. . . . I should have mentioned that I actually am married to such a 'Goy' and that one should feel as little free in my company to talk about this as one should talk absolutely 'freely' about the Jews in Heinrich's presence."[100] For Scholem solidarity entailed responsibility, and even connected criticism had its decent limits.[101] After their rift he wrote: "I knew Hannah Arendt when she was a socialist or half-communist, and I knew her when she was a Zionist. I am astounded by her ability to pronounce upon movements in which she once was so deeply engaged, in terms of a distance measured in light years and from such sovereign heights."[102]

As the years went by the gulf between the two became even greater. We should not, however, exaggerate its importance. Viewed in larger historical perspective, their differences and the intensity with which they expressed them were, I think, linked to a certain kind of kinship and flowed from some profound commonalities. Family quarrels, after all, are often the most strongly felt. Both exemplified the radical revolt against German-Jewish bourgeois modes of assimilation. Both were classical German-Jewish intellectuals, products of the European and Jewish traditions, aspects of which they subjected to the most withering critique. (This accounts in many ways, I think, for the current fascination with them in Western intellectual circles.)[103] As David Suchoff points out, both "created new models for the transmission of tradition and the relation between culture and political action. Their writing sought to confront, without repressing, the scandal that Jewish particularity posed to German culture in their period."[104]

Paradoxically, their negative personal evaluations of each other also looked like mirror images. Each regarded the other as megalomaniacally arrogant and self-obsessed.[105] As early as 1957, Arendt wrote that Scholem was "so self-preoccupied that he has no eyes (and not only that: no ears). Basically he believes: The midpoint of the world is

Israel; the midpoint of Israel is Jerusalem; the midpoint of Jerusalem is the university and the midpoint of the university is Scholem. And the worst of it is that he really believes that the world has a central point."[106] But of course, there *were* significant differences, reflected both in the making of their German-Jewish selves and their intellectual projects. Arendt's narratives did depart from Scholem's more organic, Zionist version. The twentieth-century experience of forced statelessness rendered her suspicious of all homogenizing politics, including that of Zionism. In response to these events she sought to design a disclosive politics of plurality. Scholem's achievement lay in unraveling the totality of Judaism, conceived (romantically) as an organism in which the inner logic, conflicts, and dialectics unfolded in immanent, if always open, fashion. Even if his imagined tools and categories were of European provenance, it was the world of Judaic integrity, not the European tradition, that Scholem sought to recapture. For Arendt it was the crisis of these traditions that lay at the center.

The source of her achievements, conflicts, and limitations lay in the fact that in her great engagement with the wider world, she exemplified the bifurcated Western Jew that she acutely diagnosed and critiqued. Arendt was perhaps the keenest analyst, but also the embodiment, of the experience of German-Jewish intellectuals—their conflicts and convolutions but also their immense creativity.[107] Scholem was interested in Judaism; Arendt, who knew very little about the body of Judaism itself, was the great explicator of "Jewishness" and its psychological machinations. She highlighted its ambivalences, multiple loyalties, fissures, breakdowns, and partial reconstitutions. But she did not do this only within a Jewish framework. Arendt was engaged with manifold worlds and political affiliations; she took as her starting point the individual and the rupture with tradition as such. Scholem was, of course, aware of the crisis and breakdown of tradition but concentrated upon its internal, immanent manifestations. For Arendt the fundamental datum—and great opportunity—of the age was this general breakdown, the collapse of that which had been handed down and the need to think things radically anew. This model of fracture and conflict could not sit easily with more organic national narratives, cut out of more unified, heroic materials.[108] While for Scholem this produced an impossible situation, a dead end, for Arendt the most valuable achievement of the modern German-Jewish intellectuals was that they "were led by their personal [Jewish] conflicts to a much more general and radical problem, namely, to questioning the relevance of the Western tradition as a whole."[109] This, surely, was also meant autobiographically. What ultimately was Arendt's project but the attempt to rethink the Western political and philosophical tradition at a time when all certainties, including Jewish ones, no longer seemed to possess absolute validity? "I sit (happily) between two stools," she wrote to Kurt Blumenfeld in 1952, "see . . . the foundations totter and break my head over this—and read philosophy from Plato to Nietzsche to find out why the West never actually had a decent political philosophy; or the other way around, why the great tradition is dumb, silent when we ask our questions."[110] Her performative "thinking without bannisters" necessarily entailed a disclosive complexity of Jewish selfhood and its intermingling within an inescapably plural world.

If Scholem turned his ideological back on Europe and Arendt sought to radically rethink its legacy, Victor Klemperer was its great defender, especially as the Nazi darkness descended. While Scholem defined himself through a strictly Jewish prism and Arendt dissented from all "essentialist," nationalist forms of identification, Klemperer stood (at least initially) as the great defender of the promise of Enlightened *Deutschtum*, Germanism, and as the fervent advocate of assimilation. It is to his dramatic chronicles, and the logic (and collapse?) of the alternative that he proposed that we turn in the next chapter.

3

Victor
Klemperer

And the Shock

of Multiple

Identities

In 1968 Hannah Arendt published a study of exemplary lives under the self-explanatory title *Men in Dark Times.*[1] Victor Klemperer does not figure there, although he would have been a most fitting subject. Arendt did not know, indeed it appears—somewhat strangely—did not even know of, Klemperer.[2] This is to be regretted, for Klemperer must be considered *the* pioneer of the study of totalitarian language, perhaps to this day one of its most insightful analysts. Arendt's 1951 *The Origins of Totalitarianism* does not mention, but would have been immeasurably enriched by, Klemperer's *LTI—Notebook of a Philologist,* which had appeared in 1947.[3] Klemperer was able to publish the book very quickly after the war because it represented the fruit of reflections that a fascinated and repelled Klemperer had made firsthand and systematically recorded in his diary throughout the Nazi years. LTI—*Lingua Tertii Imperii*—was the coded term Klemperer used at the time for "the language of the Third Reich."[4] This marvelously personal,[5] richly nuanced study of the content, structure, and corrupting dynamics of the German language under Nazism is no doubt a classic; yet strangely enough, it has remained, until recently, relatively neglected.[6]

Arendt, of course, could not possibly have known about Klemperer's diaries as they appeared many years after her death. In unique and detailed fashion they document and illuminate the unfolding of dark times in Germany under Nazism. Their recent publication, covering both National Socialism[7] and the period of the Weimar Republic,[8] has already rescued Klemperer from his previous obscurity. In this respect, his case is quite different from that of both Scholem and Arendt. Interest in their letters and diaries derives from our familiarity with their thought and published writings; with Klemperer it is the diaries themselves that have drawn attention and that may now generate interest in his other work.[9]

The diaries were widely acclaimed, became a major best seller, and brought immediate fame to Klemperer in Germany when they appeared in the mid-1990s.[10] Some critics have argued that there may be some disturbing reasons for this enthusiastic reception. After all, for all the suffering and persecution they endured, Klemperer and his wife *survived* the Third Reich and, indeed, experienced, from fellow Germans, occasional gestures of compassion, each of which Klemperer carefully noted. Because his wife, Eva, was a Protestant, they were spared the ultimacy of the death camps. As Paolo Traverso has perceptively noted, the popularity of the diaries in Germany —like those of Anne Frank (which break off at the moment of deportation and extermination)—derives from the fact that they remain within the bounds of the comprehensible. They are still somehow contained within the codes of everyday life, not entirely removed from the realm of private, bourgeois experience. They record, in the face of incredible odds, the maintenance and triumph of human values.[11] They provide a distraction from the greater, total horror, as well as an alternative to the picture of an unrelieved, deeply ingrained, and inexorably *murderous* popular German antisemitism that Daniel Goldhagen presented in Germany at roughly the same time.[12] Like *Schindler's List*, Klemperer's diary contains at least some good Germans and a happy ending.

It should be clear, however, that the possible misuse of these documents in no way detracts from their immense documentary value. They are particularly relevant in our context. In the first place, Klemperer records and illuminates public life, the epoch-making events and atmosphere of his times, from a most personal perspective and in remarkably detailed, quotidian, humanizing fashion. The difficulties and humiliations as well as the absurdities that confronted a Jew living in prewar Nazi Germany are poignantly brought home. The diaries record, in painstaking yet compelling detail, the enormous problems created, for instance, by the everyday tasks of maintaining a car and a garden or building a house. In this context such normally innocuous matters become charged, almost surreal activities. With the wisdom of hindsight one may well ask which Jew in the Third Reich would be obsessed with keeping a garden, learning to drive, building a house? But, of course, given both Klemperer's objective situation and his ideological outlook, this was an essential part of his insoluble dilemma.

More than in either Scholem or Arendt, public life and intimate chronicle become one in Klemperer. On the face of it, there is something obsessive, deeply egocentric, about Klemperer's graphomanic reflex of everyday record-keeping. His Weimar diaries are fittingly titled *Collecting Life, Not Asking What For and Why.* Together, the diaries (including those he wrote for the post-Nazi period)[13] and the massive two-volume autobiographical memoir, *Curriculum Vitae,*[14] also composed under Nazism and covering the years from his birth in 1881 through 1918, total many thousands of pages. The diaries for the years 1918–32 alone come to well over sixteen hundred pages. Yet, we have every reason to be grateful for this inveterate tendency to diarize. By 1933, such chronicling had become a well-established habit, part of Klemperer's everyday routine. It was not just egoism but also the discipline and honed skill of an articulate scholar combined with a growing realization that his testimony and experience—if he and/or it survived—would be of crucial historical importance, that rendered such a detailed document possible. "I shall," he wrote, "bear witness." This is a history of the Third Reich as experienced by a shrewd, yet bewildered, observer and victim, a converted Jew who survived precariously in a mixed marriage. It graphically brings to life the everyday fear, uncertainties, confusions, growing isolation, humiliations, impoverishment, and expectation of death that characterized the experience of an anomalous group of Jews—those in *Mischehen*—who somehow hung on and survived the nightmare.

Although it cannot be our main concern here, the diaries throw light, among other things, on the vexed question of German popular opinion from 1933 to 1945. Klemperer was constantly testing these waters—albeit in a random and occasional, rather than scientific, way. After all, issues such as the nature and extent of support for the Nazis and their policies, the degree of popular antisemitism, were, for Klemperer, not academic matters but indices and guides to his prospects for survival. No clear-cut picture emerges—inhumanity exists side by side with jokes critical of the regime and moving expressions of decency. The diaries are dotted with such examples. Thus, the person who in 1938 had to inform Klemperer that he had been banned from using the library is introduced as follows: "The man [an old *Stahlhelm* man!] was distressed beyond words, I had to calm him. He stroked my hand the whole time, he could not hold back the tears, he stammered: I am boiling over inside."[15]

Still, the brooding presence of the regime and the sense of its awesome power are overwhelming. Klemperer is particularly keen at noting the built-in ambivalences, the difficulties of judgment. Thus, he reports a policeman's vacillation "between the roughness he had been ordered to display and respect and sympathy"[16] and reports of acquaintances: "They are not Nazis, and are very fond of us, but the Fuehrer's picture hangs in the pharmacy."[17] Klemperer, too—for perfectly understandable reasons—constantly vacillates. "Each of us wants to fathom the mood of the people and is dependent on the last remark picked up from the barber or butcher."[18] At some moments (as in March 1940) he asks himself "where all the wild anti-Semitism is. For my part, I encounter much sympathy, people help me out, but fearfully of course."[19] Yet, paradoxically, much earlier (in 1936) he concludes that "the NSDAP has assessed the popular mood quite accurately and that the Jewish dream of being German has been a dream after all. That is the most bitter truth for me."[20] And, later, of the *Kristallnacht* pogroms, he commented that they "made less impression on the nation than cutting the bar of chocolate for Christmas."[21]

Klemperer's notes from the inside, moreover, are exceedingly useful in clarifying the perennial question of how much was known about Nazi atrocities. Despite

the fact that he was confined to the *Judenhaus,* in which
mixed couples were forced to live, and despite his feelings
of isolation and ignorance,[22] the extent and accuracy of
Klemperer's knowledge—acquired through rumor, foreign radio broadcasts, and other means—is remarkable
and casts considerable doubt upon subsequent claims that
Germans (more fortunate than him) were quite unaware
of what was transpiring. Throughout the course of the
Third Reich Klemperer hears about and reports on the
camps—from Buchenwald to Theresienstadt.[23] He is aware
of the deportations to Poland[24] and reports in May 1941
on the euthanasia program: "Sonnenstein has long ceased
to be the regional mental asylum. The SS is in charge.
They have built a special crematorium. Those who are not
wanted are taken up in a kind of police van. People here
call it the 'whispering coach.' Afterwards the relatives receive the urn."[25] As early as mid-March 1942 he knows
of the existence of Auschwitz, "the most horrible of the
camps."[26] That April—over a glass of beer in a local pub
in Dresden—his Aryan wife is told by someone who had
served in a police battalion in Russia about the "gruesome
mass murders of Jews in Kiev. Small children whose heads
were smashed against the wall, men, women and half-
grown-ups in their thousands massed together . . . and
masses of corpses buried under exploded earth."[27] Indeed,
over the course of the diary, Auschwitz becomes a familiar
landmark,[28] mentioned in an almost matter-of-fact way.[29]
In May 1943 he quotes from literature (in this case an
article published by Johann von Leers) that openly pro-
claims the need to exterminate the Jews.[30] Long before
the conclusion of the war, Klemperer astutely sought to
explicate the special methods and nature of the crime. In
August 1942 he declared: "There is nothing spontaneous
here, it is methodically organised and designed, it is 'cul-

tivated' atrocity, and it is happening, hypocritically, in the name of culture. . . . *We* do not simply murder."[31] By October 1944, Klemperer not only knew of the mass killings being perpetrated as the Germans retreated but, through various sources, was able to venture a succinct assessment of the event as a whole: "six to seven million Jews (out of the fifteen that had existed), have been slaughtered (more precisely: shot and gassed)."[32]

The diaries become even more fascinating and relevant for the purposes of our own theme because—in the face of an unprecedentedly brutal political reality—they chronicle in strikingly immediate fashion the shock, the gradual undoing of a world; the collapse of an ideology; the threats to an (already fragile) identity; and the manifold, ongoing attempts to somehow rationalize or hold on to and then, later, confront older positions and attitudes and—in various ways—to rethink set postures and create new possibilities of identity.

This is a peculiarly twentieth-century experience, a *Bildungsroman* in which, like it or not, the sheer humanity of the man—the vulnerabilities[33] and unexpected strength, fear, insatiable curiosity, hypochondria, honesty, foibles, opportunism, and capacity for self-examination[34]—is revealed as much to the author as the reader. I say "like it or not" advisedly. For if anyone seems to embody the "negative" post–World War II archetype of "the German Jew"—deeply assimilationist; a convert to Protestantism; almost ecstatically committed to, and blinded by, his *Deutschtum* (Germanness); obsessively anti-Zionist—it is Klemperer. If for Scholem the turn to Zionism was almost instinctive, so too was Klemperer's initial recoil from it. And if Arendt, politely but firmly, declined Jaspers's plea to regard her as "a German," Klemperer would have welcomed this with open arms. Scholem and Arendt were a generation or so younger and might well have viewed Klemperer with a disdain bordering on contempt.

It is not irrelevant to note that Klemperer, born in 1881 in Landsberg in the Warthe, was the son of a provincial, (very) Reform rabbi who, as part of his full identification as a *Reichsdeutscher*, called himself a "preacher" (*Prediger*), not a rabbi.[35] As Klemperer puts it in his memoirs (painfully relived and written under Nazi rule), it never occurred to his father that there could be a conflict between *Deutschtum* and *Judentum*. Not surprisingly, Jewish religious substance was endowed with an entirely universal and abstract import, and external ritual and cult were strongly devalued. After swearing the Hitler oath in 1933—for purely opportunistic career reasons that ultimately did not help in any case—Klemperer bitterly regretted his youthful upbraiding of his father for eating breakfast on Yom Kippur.[36] (Like many pre–World War I young Jews—most prominently Kafka[37]—both Scholem and Klemperer were very much aware of the emptiness of their religious education although, of course, they responded in radically antithetical ways.) At any rate, with its German-speaking, organ-playing, hatless, mixed, Sunday services, Klemperer writes, Reform constituted "the most radical expression of the will to *Deutschtum*."[38] Typically, his brother Georg closely supervised his mastery of High German; and while he was allowed occasional lapses into a Berlin accent, nothing even vaguely Yiddish-sounding was acceptable.[39] For his part, Klemperer enthusiastically adopted these values. Jewish "separatism" of any sort was rejected and, regardless of the obstacles of integration (of which he was aware), he enthusiastically and naturally appropriated German ways. As he put it, "I did not feel myself to be a Jew, not even a German Jew, but rather purely and simply a German."[40]

Of course, Klemperer envisaged the content of this Germanness in very specific, highly selective ways.[41] Germanism was simply equated with a kind of Enlightened Protestantism: "I always took [Gotthold Ephraim] Lessing's thought to be Protestant,"[42] he proclaimed. Indeed, as late as February 1943, Klemperer defended Lessing's dogma-free Protestant version of Christianity as the ideal.[43] Klemperer not only admired Lessing, he often took the wise philosopher's words and adapted them to his situation. Thus, when a Gentile friend showed no real comprehension of what dreadful things were happening in Nazi Germany and claimed that one could "still be a Nazi for idealistic reasons, without being a criminal or an idiot," he retorted: "I changed Lessing's words—Anyone who does not lose his reason over certain things, has no reason —into: Anyone whose heart remains calm today, has no heart. She departed stricken."[44] That Klemperer so revered Lessing, Moses Mendelssohn's friend and defender, should come as no surprise. This Enlightenment figure was an icon of educated German Jewry[45]—admired, incidentally, as much by Arendt[46] as by Klemperer.

In this respect, at least, despite or even because of his earlier apostasy, Klemperer was a classical *Bildungs*-Jew, with all the strengths and weaknesses famously depicted in another Efroymson lecture series by George Mosse.[47] Whether or not Klemperer recognized this irony, his special affinity for France and its culture, home of the Enlightenment, was typical of a broader acculturated liberal Jewish impulse.[48] After a brief, unsuccessful attempt at a commercial career, Klemperer became a literary critic and a (rather frustrated) professor of Romance language and literature—a choice of field that flowed quite naturally from this *Bildungs*-sensibility. Like so many other German-Jewish intellectuals, Klemperer was by temperament a cultivated liberal-humanist and essentially an apolitical creature (until circumstances forced him in a different direction). He enunciated this sensibility in an almost classic way in a 1919 entry: "I will vote for the Democrats. . . . A liberal cannot rule. For he represents the individual and ruling means to think in terms of masses. But I will not give up. The proletarian feels himself to be a part of the mass, the Social Democrat represents him. I feel myself as an Individual. The Liberals will not get to rule, but here and there they intervene to moderate things for the individual. . . . The Liberal is the yeast in the kitchen."[49]

These generally were the preferences of German-Jewish intellectuals. To a great degree, liberal self-cultivation, culture, ideas, curiosity, the world of learning and understanding for its own humanizing sake constituted Klemperer's world—as indeed (albeit in different ways) it did for Scholem and Arendt. It was characteristic that in the prewar era Klemperer would attend political meetings not because he had any interest in the politics but because he was fascinated by the nature and forms of the rhetoric.[50] Is it such a surprise, then, that the definitive study of the uses—and especially the abuses—of the German language under the Nazis should have been written by this *Bildungs*-German Jew beyond Judaism? (The degree to which *converted* German-speaking Jews in particular were sensitive to the duplicities and power, the limits and possibilities, of language is striking. One need point here only to Karl Kraus and Ludwig Wittgenstein.)

Ritchie Robertson has written recently that admirable as this love of books and culture may have been among German-Jewish intellectuals, it could be excessive, the priority given to the life of the mind disproportionate.[51] In Klemperer's case under the Third Reich, however, it not only provided him with an analytic eye, crucial to the work of serious chronicling, it was literally life-saving. In an age of barbarism, his work, his reading, plunging into obscure and famous works, especially of eighteenth-century French literature, and, indeed, the very act of diarizing, provided him with a refuge, an outlet, consolation, meaning.[52] Just this belief in the spirit and power of ideas prompted him to note of its betrayers in August 1936: "If one day the situation were reversed and the fate of the vanquished lay in my hands, then I would let all the ordinary folk go and even some of the leaders. . . . But I would have all the intellectuals strung up, and the professors three feet higher than the rest."[53]

The connection in Klemperer's life between Germanism, Protestantism, and Enlightenment was, of course, always a fragile construction. Like so many other things, his relationship to Protestantism could be ambiguous[54] and changed considerably over time. Indeed, he converted twice (once for instrumental reasons and once out of conviction); after the war,[55] given what he considered to be the unforgivable attitude of Protestantism under the Nazis, he left the church completely.[56] What never wavered was his relationship to his Protestant wife, Eva (née Schlemmer), a pianist and musicologist. This was an extraordinary intimacy. Klemperer was throughout acutely aware of the extraordinary nature of their relationship. Well before the rise of the Nazis to power he noted in his diary: "I was immediately destined for, and belonged to, Eva, bodily, spiritually, in everything; and it has so remained. My whole life, really my whole life, from the beginning of my serious life—*she* was the beginning—lies in this being together with Eva."[57] Despite the horrible indignities, the harrowing humiliations, the mental and physical sufferings and deprivations that she endured on account of her husband's Jewish origins, in all the diaries for this period, astonishingly, there is not a single word, not a hint, of resentment or anger, no suggestion of separation. This may, of course, be a naive reading. Perhaps Eva's instability, her constant illnesses and depressions, were coded forms for expressing this anger. But the point remains—if such resentment indeed existed, it was highly sublimated.[58] What is certain is the fact that Klemperer survived only because he was intermarried—he was quite aware that he owed his life to Eva.[59]

Indeed, 98 percent of German Jews who survived the war were from such mixed marriages. What is surprising is the fact that the Klemperers were typical rather than exceptional. Although the couple is omitted, rather strangely, from a valuable study on the topic, Nathan Stoltzfus has demonstrated that despite the enormous pressures exerted toward separation and divorce by the regime, these marriages were notably resilient. The integration of German Jews into German society—at least in some sectors—was much tighter than we might have thought. Remarkably, in 1933, quite against the grain of the new politics, the rate of mixed marriages was as high as 44 percent, though by 1934 it had dropped to 15 percent, a still rather amazing figure. In June 1935, thirty-five thousand of the five hundred thousand Jews in Germany lived in such intermarriages. The Nuremberg Laws prevented future intermarriages but did not nullify existing ones. But, of course, this atmosphere was designed to encourage divorce. While prior to 1935 some couples did indeed turn to divorce, others, amazingly, rushed to marry before the law prevented it.

As time went on, Jews in such marriages were almost the only Jews left in Germany. Although they too were slated for extermination, theirs was a relatively privileged status; for though they lost their rights and citizenship, their partners did not. The majority of these were, like the Klemperers, marriages of Jewish men to non-Jewish women. One of the rare illuminations of this period was the great loyalty, fortitude, and courage of such German wives. The great Berlin Rosenstrasse demonstration of mid-1943 at which non-Jewish women successfully protested the planned deportation of their Jewish husbands was not only immensely brave but points to the unmined possibilities of protest as a limit, or at least a social restraint, on totalitarian omnipotence.[60]

Intermarriage was, of course, a mortal blow to Nazi ideology, an odious offense as well as a practical danger whereby, as Himmler complained, Germans developed feelings for Jews.[61] It took special inner powers and grace to withhold the attack from without. This was especially so for the Klemperers since theirs was classified a "simple" rather than a "privileged" intermarriage. (Karl and Gertrud Jaspers—yet another example of a bond that withstood almost unbearable pressures—belonged to the latter category.) "Privileged" intermarriages applied where the wife was Jewish or at least one child was baptized a Christian. Such unions outweighed nonprivileged marriages by three to one because overwhelmingly *Mischlinge* were baptized as Christians.[62] As a childless couple in which the male partner was Jewish, the Klemperers were disqualified on both counts. This made Eva's deportment even more admirable. Klemperer was obviously aware that he owed his life to her and not only dedicated *LTI* to her but introduced that volume by distinguishing between her genuine, selfless heroism and the bombastic, brutal, fake *Heldentum* of the Nazis. In the dedication he wrote: "For without you this book would not exist and for some time now neither its writer."[63]

The advent, the shame, of Nazism was, of course, the

major watershed in Klemperer's life. It constituted not only a crisis of personal survival but a fundamental challenge to his worldview, indeed, to his very self-definition. His diaries record in fascinating detail the ongoing attempt to grasp and analyze the implications of, and perhaps devise new defenses against and solutions to, the assaults on his ideological world. They relentlessly register the shocks to his—already somewhat fragile—identity. His identity and intellectual world were very differently constructed from those of Scholem and Arendt, whose Zionist narrative acted as a kind of ideological shock absorber, one that provided at least a modicum of intellectual self-immunization. Klemperer did have the psychological acuity to perceive that the greater the attachment to Germany and Germanism, the greater the vulnerability.[64] He was aware, too, of other ironic advantages pertaining to a positive Jewish identity in those times. As a friend pointed out to him when the danger of deportation in 1941 was imminent: "I shall . . . be a very poor and pitiable 'Yid' when I . . . am sitting in a Polish or Russian ghetto."[65] All of Klemperer's cherished beliefs, his social and philosophical presuppositions, his faith in *Deutschtum*, his positive evaluation of the Germans, his ideas about assimilation, antisemitism, Jewishness, Zionism (and more) came under an almost overwhelming barrage.

The experience of 1933 was indeed sharp and traumatic. But it would be wrong to portray the earlier Klemperer as the fully Germanized, successfully assimilated Jew in a relatively tension-free pre-Nazi German society. An abiding uneasiness renders the play and transformations of Klemperer's multiple identities even more interesting. It is in their complexities and ambivalences, not their black-and-white character, that the fascination resides. Thus, despite Klemperer's obduracy concerning his

"Germanness," as his Weimar diaries make clear, his residual Jewishness *was* a factor even then. There was no simplistic self-deception at work here. In the first place he was very much aware of the antisemitism that raged through the Republic from 1918 on and punctiliously noted such sentiments and incidents. For example, in September 1919, he reports on a conversation that gave him an "insight into the horrible Jewish agitation that is shamelessly and threateningly being conducted throughout Germany. It is frightening. No one here takes me for a Jew. Good people, educated people and so susceptible to this crazy agitation. It is frightening. The Jew is guilty of everything: the war, the revolution, Bolshevism, capitalism, everything. Enlighten them and they see it, but certainly tomorrow they are roused again."[66] His Jewishness, moreover, constituted an ongoing obstacle to obtaining a prestigious position—his academic career was a most frustrating one and the post he eventually obtained at the Dresden Technical University was not exactly the pinnacle of German academia.[67] There too he encountered the antisemitism among students and faculty that was so pervasive in the Weimar Republic.[68]

But the connections were not only external. Psychologically they went deeper than that. Thus Klemperer reports on his discomfort when, on the one hand, various Jews made derogatory comments on his Protestant apostasy, his conversion and betrayal,[69] and on the other hand, when keeping silent about his own Jewishness: "It is often painful to me that people do not seem to know of my Jewish origins. Once, I will have to be open about this. But when will be the right time for that?"[70]

Yet Klemperer was also very much aware that many of his contemporaries *did* continue to regard him as a Jew. To depict him as entirely self-deceived, unaware of his surroundings, would be absurd in light of numerous shrewd interpersonal analyses (such as the following with a senior fellow academic): "I flattered him, he was courteous, we conducted ourselves in a friendly manner. But with that we knew exactly where we stand with each other. For him I am the Jew, for me he is the surviving potentate whose place I would gladly take."[71] Klemperer shared the prejudice that Jews were inevitably clever (as evidenced by his shock upon meeting a particularly stupid one).[72] From time to time he even recorded how impressed he was with the ongoing energy of Judaism as it still manifested itself in various areas of life: from the traditional Jewish quarter in Amsterdam to the remarkable Jewish influence—via Bergson and Proust—on modern French literature.[73] Indeed, well before the rise of the Nazis, there were moments when he was plagued by what today would be called an "identity crisis." "And now," he wrote in August 1927, "everything in Germany pushes me back to the Jews. But if I became a Zionist I would be even more laughable than if I were to become a Catholic. I am always suspended, like an aeroplane, over these things and myself. That is incidentally the most Jewish thing about me. And perhaps the most German. But the German nevertheless finds somewhere a unity of feeling. The Jew remains also above his feeling."[74]

Certainly, when it came to the dynamics of intimacy, Jewishness remained very much a conscious factor. He continued to feel more at home, more at ease, with Jewish friends of his own kind rather than of the Orthodox or Zionist or *ostjüdische* kind.[75] Thus his comments about a visit from a distant relative, Dr. Ralf von Klemperer: "We talked about antisemitism, about our studies, etc. No flaunting, no false Christians, no pushy Judaism, naturalness."[76] Klemperer even reports that the atmosphere of an evening became more relaxed once "foreign bodies" (*nichtjüdische Fremdkörper*)—Gentile acquaintances—had departed.[77] On another occasion he commented: "We chatted till three. We understood each other well. Jewish blood— that's a thing of its own [*es ist nun einmal ein Ding für sich*]."[78] Gershom Scholem once commented that in order for Jewish-Gentile intimacy to occur, the Gentile needed somehow to be "verjudet" [Judaized]:[79] how ironic and surprising it is to read that in her leisure time, Eva successfully wrestled with crossword puzzles spiced with Yiddish expressions.[80]

Moreover, the political content of Klemperer's Germanness was not always the lofty Enlightenment version of humanity and culture that he later advocated: a front volunteer of 1915, his attitudes to World War I and to Germany's enemies were conventionally and chauvinistically nationalist.[81] In December 1918—admittedly in opposition to revolutionary violence and antisemitic populist attitudes—he declared (he must have lived to have deeply regretted this statement): "Democracy in any form is far more stupid than despotism. Stupid is not the correct word: it is more mendacious, mean, dumber, senseless, unjust."[82] Later, he constantly equated Rousseau, that creature of the French Enlightenment, with Hitler.[83] (This was not all that strange. We should not forget that for Jacob Talmon, the Israeli historian, Rousseau was the definitive father of the totalitarian democracy of the left.)[84] Moreover, Klemperer had words of praise—though qualified— and understanding for Maurice Barres, the French proto-Fascist.[85] (Parenthetically, we should note that, albeit for different reasons, both Scholem and Arendt were themselves, and for a far longer time, critics of liberalism and the Enlightenment.) Klemperer's Weimar diaries often record his regrets that only the antisemitism of the right precluded him from making this his political home.[86] Like most of us, Klemperer could not rid himself easily of visual stereotypes: "Goebbels," he wrote, "looks uncommonly Jewish."[87] And this great critic of totalitarian thinking and prejudicial generalizations was earlier a firm believer in "national character," a practitioner of "Völkerpsychologie" and group essences—in which, inevitably, the German case was presented as the ideal standard.[88] And, at the beginning, even his critique of the regime, his "feeling of disgust and shame," was formulated in a quasi-racist way: "We would be more likely to live in a state of law under French negro occupation than under this government."[89]

But this does change, though at times in an ambivalent, conflicted way. In April 1933 Klemperer writes: "I am unable to work on my 'Image of France' [project]. I no longer believe in national psychology. Everything that I held to be unGerman, brutality, injustice, deception, mass suggestion to the point of intoxication, all of it is flourishing here."[90] And it is in these dark years that his unequivocal commitment to the Enlightenment ripens. Leafing through his beloved Lessing's *Nathan the Wise,* it is not the philo-semitism that impresses him "but the sentence: 'What does a nation mean after all?'—I myself have had too much nationalism in me and am now punished for it."[91] And even more strongly and famously he writes in 1938: "I am definitively changed . . . my nationalism and patriotism are gone forever. Every national circumscription appears barbarous to me. My thinking is now completely a Voltairean cosmopolitanism . . . Voltaire and Montesquieu are more than ever my essential guides."[92] Yet, significantly, Klemperer prefaced these words with the declaration that: "No one can take my Germanness from me."

Indeed, perhaps not so ironically (for what was previously a reflex had to become exquisitely self-conscious), his commitment to, and interpretations of, *Deutschtum* now become far more explicitly omnipresent and thoroughly, if idiosyncratically, thought through. When considering emigration in 1933, Klemperer declares that he can only teach "in German and from a completely German perspective. I must live and die here."[93] (It should be pointed out that the reasons for Klemperer's remaining in Germany were as much related to practical difficulties as they were to ideological considerations.) The diaries reveal a strategy of splitting. The simultaneous commitment to *Deutschtum* as a spiritual, regulative idea and the disillusionment with its practical Nazi manifestations exist side by side from the very beginning. Thus, his reply to a previously assimilated Jew who felt at home in Jerusalem: "I am German forever." When it was pointed out to him that the Nazis would not concede this, Klemperer shot back: "The Nazis are unGerman."[94] As late as 1939, he protested that he could as little get along with Zionism and Bolshevism (later, ironically, he was to join the Communist Party) as he could with National Socialism. He was, he declared, "Liberal and German *forever*,"[95] even though he had proclaimed in October 1937 that from the perspective of present circumstances, the entry of the Jews "into *Deutschtum*, their role in liberalism . . . is shattered."[96]

Certainly Klemperer did not shut his eyes to the new, empirical reality. Already in the Weimar diaries he closely and perceptively followed the rise of fascist tendencies.[97] Rather presciently he observed in 1920 that "Germany is now alive only as an idea; as something in the present (*Gegenwärtiges*) it is in all its parts equally loathsome."[98] And early in 1933 he wrote "I feel shame more than fear, shame for Germany. I have truly always felt myself a

German. I have always imagined: the 20th century and Mitteleuropa was different from the 14th century and Romania. Mistake."[99] By 1937 he had become much more blunt: "There is so much lethargy in the German people and so much immorality and above all so much stupidity."[100] Moreover, he concluded, the Nazis did indeed "express the true opinion of the German people. . . . Hitler really does embody [its] soul."[101] Later he noted: "Who among the 'Aryan' Germans is really untouched by National Socialism? The contagion rages in all of them, perhaps it is not a contagion, but basic German nature."[102] By 1938 he opines (though this remained in conflict with his ongoing belief in *Deutschtum* as some kind of open regulative ideal): "I could never again trust anyone in Germany, never again feel myself uninhibitedly to be German."[103] In this same year, Klemperer indulges in a kind of Scholemian self-analysis: "How unbelievably I have deceived myself my whole life long, when I imagined myself to belong to Germany, and how completely homeless I am."[104] By June 1942, in deep despair, he declares that he can no longer defend the notion that National Socialism is an un-German matter: "It is an indigenous German growth, a carcinoma of *German* flesh."[105] Germany's soul, he cried out, "is lost in time and for eternity."[106]

And yet the longing, the desire for identification, lingered: the hope for a return of his pristine *Deutschtum* ideal remains, interspersed throughout the diaries. What he wrote in 1938 could apply, at least to a part of himself, throughout: "How beautiful Germany would be if one could still feel German and feel proud as a German."[107]

Klemperer, of course, had for a long time been aware of the divide. He had even formulated his response well before the rise of Hitler. In August 1930 he had cried out: "Here Jews—there Aryans. And where do I stand? Where

are the many who are *spiritually, intellectually* German
(*geistig deutsch*)?" (his italics)[108] Yet, the "natural" Scholemian solution to this dilemma—deepening the sense of
one's own Jewishness and committing oneself to it—
was for Klemperer, at best, only a very half-hearted option. Jewishness remained, in Klemperer's mind, indelibly
linked with separatism, narrowness, "horrible ghetto op-
pressiveness."[109] Though circumstances forced him into
some kind of identification—July 1940 was the first time
in his life that he attended an Orthodox Jewish funeral[110]
—he was never comfortable with this. "Where do I belong?" he asks plaintively in 1935. "To the Jewish nation'
decrees Hitler. And I feel the Jewish nation . . . is a comedy
and am nothing but a German or German European."[111]

As time progressed and Klemperer was confined to
the Judenhaus, there *were* moments of apparent transformation. In April 1941 he echoed, to some degree, Arendt's
logic that under conditions of persecution one resists in
terms of the identity under attack; he exclaimed: "Once I
would have said: I do not judge as a Jew. . . . Now: Yes, I
judge as a Jew, because as such I am particularly affected
by the Jewish business in Hitlerism, and because it is central to the whole structure, to the whole character of
National Socialism and is uncharacteristic of everything
else."[112] Indeed, Klemperer throughout the diaries diagnosed antisemitism as the very core, the driving, animat-
ing force behind Nazism.[113]

Circumstances were also such that Klemperer increasingly exposed himself to a virtual library of Jewish literature. Franz Rosenzweig he found baffling but occasionally revelatory;[114] he was sickened by the *völkisch*
Martin Buber[115] and impressed by the historian Simon
Dubnow;[116] he even read and appreciated, but declined to
follow, the Zionist satirist Sammy Gronemann.[117] His read-

ing sometimes led to surprising re-evaluations, a new kind of self-knowledge. Thus, in 1942 he read Ismar Elbogen's *History of the Jews in Germany*. (Elbogen, incidentally, was the brother-in-law of Klemperer's musical, highly unstable, and later very famous cousin Otto.)[118] He was shattered to discover there how thin the historical grounding of his *Deutschtum* was. He had known little of the fact that only in the very recent past Jews had acquired equal rights, little of the deep-rootedness of a Hitlerian kind of antisemitism. "Perhaps," he wrote honestly, "I had not wanted to know all of this." For all that, what he immediately added represented a serious limit to his Jewish engagement: "But despite this: I *think German*, I *am* German —I did not give this to myself, I cannot rip it out. What is tradition? Everything begins with *me*."[119] Where, he asked, could the assimilated generation turn? One could not go backwards, to Zion. *Deutschtum* (at least as Klemperer conceived it)—for all the confusions and critical disavowals—remained the central value. No wonder then that Klemperer's favorite "Jewish" author was Karl Emil Franzos, author of the famous "Halb-Asien" stories, which portrayed the salvation of (a rather backward) East European Jewry in terms of German *Bildung* and acculturation.[120]

Klemperer's relationship to Zionism represents an even more extreme example of his complex relationship to Jewishness. It is revealingly obsessive, even bizarre, and later only slightly softened. Even in the early Weimar period he compares the Zionists with the Nazis.[121] With the National Socialist assumption of power, the equation becomes ever more insistent. Zionism, with its separatist, nationalist mode of thinking, he noted, was "hateful . . . for it justifies Hitler and prepared the way for him."[122] It may be that the extremity of Klemperer's stance toward

Zionism acted as a kind of negative foil to his equally
obsessive insistence upon positively reconstituting *Deutschtum*—as Nazism increasingly became the prevailing reality.

Of the new-found interest in Palestine he wrote in
1933: "Anyone who goes there exchanges nationalism
and narrowness for nationalism and narrowness."[123] During this time, Klemperer showed not the slightest interest
in deepening his understanding of the historical and existential forces behind this movement. To him it simply
represented the Jewish counterpart to Nazism.[124] "In Zion
the Aryan is exactly in the position of the Jew here . . .
the Zionists are just as offensive as the Nazis. With their
nosing after blood, their ancient 'cultural roots,' their . . .
winding back of the world they are altogether a match for
the National Socialists."[125] The need to regard the two as
identical the further one proceeds into the dark heart of
the Third Reich becomes grotesque. In March 1942 he
announces that two things interest him: the nature of
Nazism and the history of Zionism.[126] "The Zionist Bol-
shevists," he writes in May 1942, "are the purest National
Socialists!"[127]

Klemperer's initial hostility to Herzl is almost vio-
lent. The first mention in the diaries reports a conversation in which it is claimed that Herzl's "racial theory is the
Nazi's source, not the other way round."[128] Upon studying
Herzl's writings, he declares that they contain the closest
affinities with Hitlerism.[129] Even if blood-definitions were
absent, they contained the same modes of thought, sometimes the same words, the same fanaticism.[130] As late as
July 1942, aware of the magnitude of Nazi anti-Jewish
actions, he sees as his most important task the undertaking of a more systematic Herzl-Hitler comparison.[131]

The only relatively small chink in this anti-Zionist armor appears in January 1942 when Klemperer, moved by Shmaryahu Levin's memoirs, records that for the first time it occurs to him that *"Zionism is humanism"*[132] (his italics). However, this virulently anti-Zionist animus continued throughout as evidenced in his later diaries and the chapter entitled "Zion" in *LTI*. It is true that there Klemperer did point out some of the differences between Nazism and Zionism. Herzl, he wrote, was no fanatic, but spiritually sensitive and educated. Hitler came out of the darker sources of German romanticism; Herzl's model was Wilhelm II, whom Hitler despised. Herzl never dreamed of eliminating foreign nations, never preached chosenness, and had no desire to dominate those whom he would never call lower peoples and races. All he sought were rights for a persecuted people and a modest space for them to dwell—to give the unemancipated, driven East European Jewish masses a home. (Herzl would never have employed the term *Untermensch*, except to compassionately describe the appalling treatment of Galician Jews.)[133] Still, the overwhelming impression was highly critical, and Klemperer certainly emphasized what he took to be the negative affinities as well: an identical exclusionism, the feel for, and emphasis upon, masses and mass psychology; the belief in, and exploitation of, myths and symbols and so on. Indeed, Klemperer was furious when, in the late 1940s, pro-Zionist sentiment within German communist circles (led by the redoubtable Paul Merker) insisted that after the first edition of *LTI* the chapter on "Zion" be left out. When the antisemitic, anti-Zionist purges of the 1950s led to Merker's brutal removal and, in the changed atmosphere, the "Zion" chapter was allowed to stand, a remarkably insensitive Klemperer voiced his delight and regarded his own ideas as vindicated.[134]

If Klemperer never revised his views on Zionism

this was hardly true for communism. After the war he joined the party, despite the fact that he had consistently equated Bolshevism with Nazism.[135] He had previously argued that both were "materialistic and tyrannical, both disregard and negate the freedom of the spirit and of the individual."[136] Even early on, however, he did make some distinctions (albeit not always very complimentary ones). By 1936, though he wrote that both movements repelled him, "the racial idea of National Socialism seems to me the most bestial (in the literal sense of the word)."[137] In 1941 he wrote: "We now have pure Communism. But Communism murders more honestly."[138] And as late as January 1945 he bitingly characterized as Bolshevik all those who were raising the communist scare.[139]

Klemperer's postwar diaries do provide tantalizing indications as to why, on the one hand, he left the Protestant church and, on the other, joined the Communist Party. These decisions were based on a multiplicity of considerations in which self-interest, sheer opportunism, and a certain residual idealism all played an intermingled and complex role.[140] On July 30, 1945, he wrote of the church in the post-Auschwitz age: "It is more and more mysterious to me how people can still believe in the good, loving God. I now want to leave the Church that so shamelessly stabbed me."[141] Four days earlier, he wrote of his professional and political future: "I do not want to decide in purely idealistic fashion on which horse to sit, but rather coldly reckon what is best for *my* situation, *my* freedom, future work to be done, and thus which can also serve my ideal goals. Which is the correct choice? Russia? The USA? Democracy? Communism?"[142] This same complex mix was still evident as, on November 20, 1945, he was about to join the Communist Party. "Am I a coward if I do *not* join . . . am I a coward if I do join? Do I have ex-

clusively egoistic motivations for joining? No! If I must
join a party, then let it be of the least evil. . . . Only the
Communists are really pressing for a radical elimination
of the Nazis. But they will place new unfreedoms in place
of the old. . . . But I must choose my colours."[143]
Klemperer's reasons for leaving the Protestant church
and joining the communists were then clearly mixed. But
surely both were also in some way attuned to what he believed was the urgent need for a clean slate, for the radical
cleansing (moral, political, and linguistic) of the swamp
that Germany had become. Clive James has put it a little
more cynically: Klemperer turned East, he writes, "because he thought that the Nazis had exhausted the possibilities of human evil, and a different kind of tyranny
might offer hope."[144]

For us, however, the central issue is not Klemperer's
political affiliations but the need to try to assess his ideological commitments, his personal identifications, within
some kind of fair, comparative historical perspective. We
must certainly try to avoid cheap, patronizing judgments
pronounced from the comfortable heights of historical
hindsight. This indeed becomes especially unnecessary in
light of the fact that, as the diaries vividly demonstrate,
Klemperer himself was aware of and meticulously documented and assessed the various alternative postures he
could have adopted. At times he indulges in savage self-
critique: the collapse of the German ideology, his belief
in his fellow countrymen, the self-deceptions of assimilation, these are all faithfully recorded. In many ways some
of his self-reflections seem to corroborate the Scholemian
(and to some extent, the Arendtian) critique. The trans-
parencies, contradictions, and vulnerabilities of his commitments are too obvious for us to rehearse here. But we
ought to be careful. The "correct" ideological postures,

even today, are by no means clear-cut; and Klemperer ought to be seen not only within his own context but respected for the integrity of his premises.

Whether realistic or not, he remained—or circumstances increasingly made him into—a liberal, Enlightenment individualist whose supreme values (wrapped too often, admittedly, in the guise of *Deutschtum*) were the universal ones of culture and humanity. His attachment to these values, it certainly could be argued, can by no means be vitiated or nullified by the fact that brutal political powers sought to destroy them. I could not formulate it better than Klemperer himself. He wrote in April 1942: "Today a German Jew cannot write anything without placing the German-Jewish tension at the centre. But must he therefore capitulate to the opinions of the National Socialists and appropriate their language?"[145] Was his—idealized, ethereal—conception of a humanizing Germanism less valid, less worthy, than the counter-conception of (its) butchers? "I am now fighting my fiercest struggle for my *Deutschtum*," he cried in May 1942. "I must hold fast: I am German and the others are un-German. The spirit (or intellect) decides, not the blood."[146]

Too often, Klemperer argued, one's moral choices represent capitulations to the power and categories of the immoral victor. He would, I suppose, have argued that not the drive to assimilate but the illiberal refusal to accommodate such assimilation constituted the immorality, just as he claimed—prefiguring the admittedly problematic Sartrean argument—that there really was "no German or West European Jewish question. . . . The solution of the Jewish question can only be found in the deliverance from those who have invented it."[147] Embracing Jewishness, or the substitution of one exclusivism for another, perpetuated rather than solved the underlying problem.

Klemperer's enduring belief in an insufficiently problematized, overly spiritual conception of *Deutschtum* may today strike one as somewhat strange; his feverish belief in the reality of German-Jewish assimilation as almost pathetic; and his refusal to grant (Western) Jewish life and culture a dignified authenticity and autonomy as both distasteful and misguided. But the spiritual and intellectual refusal to capitulate to political brutality and the struggle to maintain the values of culture and humanity deserve our respect and consideration. At a time when it was being jettisoned all around him, Klemperer held fast to the classical vision of German *Bildung*—clung to its sense of curiosity and openness, its hunger for humanizing experience, its desire for expanding rather than contracting horizons. "We have had two conceptions of romanticism in Germany," Klemperer wrote, "the German and the Teutonic. The German proceeded into the world, into the all-human, into the spiritual and the godly, the Teutonic into narrowness and dankness, into animality and ultimately into . . . the barbaric."[148] It was the non-Jewish Germans, not Klemperer, who had regressed to their lesser selves, who had deserted their own better heritage to which he hoped, at least in his better moods, they would return. As he put it in mid-1942, perhaps patience was the simple solution: "I am German and I am waiting for the Germans to return, they have gone into hiding somewhere."[149]

In many ways, perhaps ironically, Klemperer was deeply part of German-Jewish history, and not only because he was driven by awful circumstances to become part of it. By 1933, in a radically transformed political environment, the Jews were almost the only ones to continue preaching *Bildung*-Enlightenment values. Appearances aside, Klemperer was aware, or at least increasingly came to the awareness, that he as well incarnated this German-Jewish intellectual sensibility. He put it thus in his diary on April 10, 1946: "The Jews have an eleventh commandment: it is the only one that they have never violated; it is the cause of all their suffering. It reads: 'Thy son shall learn more than thou.'"[150] Indeed, the passion for culture, the immersion in ideas, and the drive for analytic understanding of surrounding events also characterized the lives and work of Scholem and Arendt, in so many ways his mirror opposites and yet, in so many other ways, bound together by a common fate and spiritual sensibility. Their intimate chronicles document their varying responses to this common fate and the diverse roads taken to negotiate it. None of these figures can be taken as "ordinary"; yet they were all emblematic, confronting the public cataclysms of their times and forging creative—though very different—responses to dilemmas that no twentieth-century German Jew had the luxury to evade.

Notes

Translations from the German in the text
and the notes are mine unless otherwise noted.

INTRODUCTION

1. At the time the manuscript for this publication was being finalized, in April 2000, the long-promised second volume of the diaries covering the years 1918–23 most unfortunately had not appeared. 2. I owe this formulation to a conversation with Marie Louise Knott in Berlin, April 10, 2000.

3. This is my free translation of the diary entries (Adelboden, August 1, 1918–August 1, 1919), which are reproduced in Itta Shedletzky's introduction to Gershom Scholem, *Briefe I: 1914–1947* (Munich: C. H. Beck, 1994), pp. ix–x.

4. See, for instance, Wendy Wiener and George C. Rosenwald, "A Moment's Monument: The Psychology of Keeping a Diary," *Narrative Study of Lives* 1 (1993): 30–57. Of writing a diary Robert Fothergill asks: "What part in the total economy of the psyche is played by such a high degree of self-articulation and formal self-encounter? . . . For some diarists the habit is a deliberate aid to coherent self-integration; others recognize the danger of insensibly trapping themselves in the lineaments of their own self-portraits." See Fothergill's insightful *Private Chronicles: A Study of English Diaries* (London: Oxford University Press, 1974), p. 64. I thank Amos Goldberg for guiding me around the relevant literature concerning diaries and letters.

5. See letter 18, October 9, 1923, in Martin Heidegger and Karl Jaspers, *Briefwechsel 1920–1963*, ed. Walter Biemel and Hans Saner (Frankfurt am Main: Vittorio Klostermann and Munich: Piper Verlag, 1992), p. 44. Jaspers, writing in the politically sensitive year 1933, perhaps provided Heidegger's words with a different twist when he com-

mented: "If writing has the tendency to estrange, then the more so does the word bind." See letter 112, March 10, 1933, ibid., p. 150.

6. Peter Boerner writes that the obvious distinction between them notwithstanding, there is often a literal overlap as "when two partners so regularly exchange letters that it is as if they are writing diaries for each other, or also when a correspondent sends a part or whole of his diary instead of a letter." See the chapter on the "Phenomenology of the Diary" in Peter Boerner, *Tagebuch* (Stuttgart: J. B. Metzler, 1969), p. 13.

7. "It is sometimes suggested," writes Fothergill, "that the essential impulse behind all diary-writing is some form of egotism—an estimation of the First Person as disproportionately Singular. Unless diary-writing itself be taken as proof of egotism, in which case the suggestion is tautological, the case must be put rather differently. . . . there is an important difference between a serious and conscious engagement in one's own experience, and an interest in oneself as an engrossing phenomenon" (*Private Chronicles*, pp. 76–77).

8. See the useful work by Lorna Martens, *The Diary Novel* (Cambridge: Cambridge University Press, 1985), p. 3.

9. Klemperer's diaries, begun well before the rise of National Socialism to power, were indeed intensely personal and, as Susanne zur Neiden insists, originally not meant for publication. Yet, clearly, the 1933–45 diaries represent a classic case of the desire to bear witness, and witness of the most detailed kind. See zur Neiden's "Auf dem vergessenen Alltag der Tyrannei: Die Aufzeichnungen Victor Klemperers im Vergleich zur zeitgenösisschen Tagebuchliteratur," in *Im Herzen der Finsternis: Victor Klemperer als Chronist der NS-Zeit*, ed. Hannes Heer (Berlin: Aufbau-Verlag, 1997), pp. 110–21.

1. GERSHOM SCHOLEM AND THE CREATION OF JEWISH SELF-CERTITUDE

1. For Scholem's identification with many of the themes his scholarship addressed, his radicalism, and the influence of broader revolutionary, apocalyptic themes that were staple to Weimar culture in general, see "German Jews beyond *Bildung* and Liberalism: The Radical Jewish Revival in the Weimar Republic," in my *Culture and Catastrophe: German and Jewish Confrontations with National Socialism and Other Crises* (New York: New York University Press, 1996). More recently, Steven Wasserstrom has argued that Scholem (like his Eranos colleagues Mircea Eliade and Henry Corbin) "used the tools of philology, edition, and interpretation in a way that seemed somehow subordinated to a muted metatheory—if not to a covert theology." See Steven M. Wasserstrom, *Religion after Religion: Gershom Scholem, Mircea*

Eliade, and Henry Corbin at Eranos (Princeton: Princeton University Press, 1999), pp. 24–25. 2. See David Biale's *Gershom Scholem: Kabbalah and Counter-History* (Cambridge, Mass.: Harvard University Press, 1979). The full title of Alter's book is *Necessary Angels: Tradition and Modernity in Kafka, Benjamin, and Scholem* (Cambridge, Mass.: Harvard University Press and Cincinnati: Hebrew Union College Press, 1991). See too the collection edited by Peter Schäfer and Gary Smith, *Gershom Scholem. Zwischen den Disziplinen* (Frankfurt am Main: Suhrkamp Verlag, 1995).

3. On this topic (including Martin Buber's influence on this generation), see my *Brothers and Strangers: The East European Jew in German and German-Jewish Consciousness, 1800–1923* (Madison: University of Wisconsin Press, 1982 [paperback, 1999]), especially chapters 4–8.

4. Buber's 1909 lectures to the Prague Bar-Kochba are the most pertinent here. See chapters 1–3 in his *On Judaism*, ed. N. Glatzer (New York: Schocken Books, 1972); see especially pp. 16–18.

5. This is from a conversation with Heinrich Blücher (of whom more in chapter 2), the second husband of Hannah Arendt. See Blücher's letter of October 22, 1938, in Hannah Arendt, Heinrich Blücher, *Briefe 1936–1968*, ed. Lotte Köhler (Munich and Zürich: Piper Verlag, 1996), p. 88. I used the original German version as the English translation appeared after this book was in proof. See "Within Four Walls: The Correspondence Between Hannah Arendt and Heinrich Blücher, 1936–1968," ed. and with an introduction by Lotte Kohler, trans. by Peter Constantine (New York: Harcourt, 2000), 512 pp.

6. Michael Beddow, "Don't Fell the Walnut Trees: Goethe's Fears of Revolutionary Change and His Search for a 'Synthetic Vision,'" *Times Literary Supplement*, February 11, 2000, p. 3.

7. Gershom Scholem, *Tagebücher 1. Halbband 1. 1913–1917*, ed. Karlfried Gründer and Friedrich Niewöhner with Herbert Kopp-Oberstebrink (Frankfurt am Main: Jüdischer Verlag, 1995). The diaries were kept until 1923. Unfortunately, the publication of the second volume has been long delayed. Despite many efforts, I have not been able to look at a set of printer's proof.

8. The letters and diaries offer a more authentic, immediate source than the memoirs and interviews Scholem later provided. See Gershom Scholem, *Briefe I: 1914–1947*, ed. Itta Shedletzky (Munich: C. H. Beck, 1994); *Briefe II: 1948–1970*, ed. Thomas Sparr (Munich: C. H. Beck, 1995); *Briefe III: 1971–1982*, ed. Itta Shedletzky (Munich: C. H. Beck, 1999). Edited and with a fine introduction by Antony Skinner, a selection of these letters, *Gershom Scholem: A Life in Letters*, is forthcoming in English translation (Cambridge, Mass.: Harvard University Press).

9. I am assuming this to be the case, although the bracketed el-

lipses that appear throughout the diaries may consist of such sexual material, which the editors, for one reason or another, have omitted.

10. *Briefe I*, p. 80, letter 29, July 17, 1917.

11. See the diary entries for July 29, 1915, and March 8, 1916, *Tagebücher 1*, pp. 138, 283–84. I was alerted to this aspect by Michael Brenner's article "From Self-Declared Messiah to Scholar of Messianism: The Recently Published Diaries Present Young Gerhard Scholem in a New Light," *Jewish Social Studies* 3, no. 1 (Fall 1996): 177–83, especially pp. 180–81.

12. Scholem's diaries are literally peppered with his early admiration for—and his later, extremely critical view of—Buber. For the most "academic" treatment, see his "Martin Buber's Interpretation of Hasidism" in Gershom Scholem, *The Messianic Idea in Judaism and Other Essays in Jewish Spirituality* (New York: Schocken Books, 1971). Scholem's relationship to Benjamin is well known and I have thus not discussed it here. See Scholem's *Walter Benjamin: The Story of a Friendship,* trans. Harry Zohn (Philadelphia: Jewish Publication Society, 1981). He also edited and published their riveting correspondence in *The Correspondence of Walter Benjamin and Gershom Scholem, 1932–1940,* trans. Gary Smith and Andre Lefevere (New York: Schocken Books, 1989). Much of this correspondence has been superbly analyzed by Robert Alter in *Necessary Angels.*

13. *Tagebücher 1*, p. 420, entry for November 18, 1916.

14. Ibid., p. 223, entry for December 31, 1915.

15. Ibid., p. 33, entry for August 17, 1914.

16. As George Steiner put it in a general overview of Scholem's lifework: "Scholem's analytic powers were entranced, though never suborned by, the fertility of unreason in the human psyche and in history." See Steiner's *Errata: An Examined Life* (London: Phoenix Books, 1988), p. 132.

17. If the idiom, the rhetoric, the passion, the categories are Nietzschean, this is obviously a nationalized and Judaized Nietzsche. "We, who want to liberate our Volk, we who are young . . . must go to the mountains and search for God" (*Tagebücher 1*, p. 36).

18. These early ruminations belie Scholem's later repeated insistence on his distaste for Nietzsche (and Zarathustra). His remarks to Robert Alter were characteristic of this approach: "As to Nietzsche, I must confess that I feel no kinship to him or to his heritage and as a young man, I turned away in disgust from those writings of Nietzsche which came into my hands. Unfortunately, these seem to have been the wrong ones, like Zarathustra, and they prevented me from delving deeper." See *Briefe III*, p. 72, letter 70 to Alter, May 15, 1973; in the same volume see also p. 178.

19. Nietzsche appears ubiquitously in the diaries, sometimes critically but more often as an object of veneration. He writes in the diary on November 15, 1914 (*Tagebücher 1*, p. 46, freely translated): "And still I sometimes think that a great deal of Life is contained in these books. Certainly books have given me much. The Bible, Zarathustra. . . ." The entry for November 27 (ibid., p. 65) reads: "Historical connectedness. Very serious problem. Tradition, historical consciousness, Fatherland. We say with Nietzsche: The land of the child (Kinderland) is the land of the future. We must not measure or orient the future in terms of the past. For we have our ancestors' blood in us—that should give us sufficient historical connectedness. No backward return to Judaism: the romanticism of degeneration. Everything that is a great and serious danger for Zionism. Not the ancient, but mysticism that is young, is born with us." His note on September 21, 1915 (ibid., p. 160), quotes again from Zarathustra: "The stillest word brings the storm." See too the discussion on October 27, 1916 (ibid., p. 412). Some time ago, I argued the case for the Nietzschean side of Scholem but at the time lacked this supporting evidence. See "German Jews beyond *Bildung* and Liberalism," in *Culture and Catastrophe*.

20. *Tagebücher 1*, p. 207, entry for December 18, 1915.

21. Ibid., p. 52, entry for November 17, 1914.

22. Letter 64 to Aharon Heller, June 23, 1918, *Briefe I*, p. 163.

23. Scholem records these readings in his diary entry for November 17, 1914, *Tagebücher 1*, pp. 51–52.

24. Letter 58 to Werner Kraft, April 8, 1918, *Briefe I*, p. 151.

25. One of the editors of the Scholem diaries, Herbert Kopp-Oberstebrink, has elsewhere also noted Scholem's early attraction to Nietzsche, although he claims that this youthful infatuation had few significant after-effects in the thought of the more mature thinker. I would claim that many of these categorical connections remained as a kind of implicit, though crucial, undergirding. See Kopp-Oberstebrink, "Unzeitgemässe Betrachtungen zu Nietzsche contra jüdische Nietzscheanismen. Ein Kapitel aus der intellektuellen Frühgeschichte Gershom Scholems," in *Jüdische Nietzscheanismus*, ed. Werner Stegmaier and Daniel Krochmalnik (Berlin and New York: Walter de Gruyter, 1997), pp. 90–105. The qualification appears on p. 92.

26. *Tagebücher 1*, p. 33, entry for August 17, 1914.

27. "Gershom Scholem as a German Jew," in George Mosse, *Confronting the Nation: Jewish and Western Nationalism* (Hanover, N.H., and London: University Press of New England for Brandeis University Press, 1993). But see too my "German Jews beyond *Bildung* and Liberalism."

28. *Tagebücher 1*, p. 87, entry for January 29, 1915.

29. Ibid., p. 158, entry for September 19, 1915.
30. Ibid., p. 61, entry for November 26, 1914.
31. Ibid., p. 112, entry for January 27, 1915. See, too, the discussion by Ritchie Robertson in his excellent *The 'Jewish Question' in German Literature, 1749–1939: Emancipation and Its Discontents* (Oxford: Oxford University Press, 1999), p. 392.
32. *Tagebücher 1*, p. 116, entry for May 22, 1915.
33. Ibid., p. 119, entry for May 22, 1915.
34. Not surprisingly the diaries are filled with references to Stefan George and his circle (see *Tagebücher 1*, pp. 43, 46, 63, 71, 80, 94, 118–19, 141, 170–73, 175, 286–87, 364, 390, 444).
35. On the George-Nietzsche relationship as formulated by the poet and his followers, see my *The Nietzsche Legacy in Germany, 1890–1990* (Berkeley: University of California Press, 1992), pp. 4, 21, 71–83, 118, 125, 140–41, 308.
36. *Tagebücher 1*, pp. 120–21, entry for May 22, 1915. "Shalem" in Hebrew means whole, perfect.
37. I owe this formulation to Kenneth Seeskin.
38. *Tagebücher*, p. 158, entry for September 19, 1915.
39. See Michael Brenner, "From Self-Declared Messiah to Scholar of Messianism: The Recently Published Diaries Present Young Gerhard Scholem in a New Light," *Jewish Social Studies* 3, no. 1 (Fall 1996): 177–83, especially pp. 178–79.
40. Scholem's attitude to those who sought to link the personal with the scholarly was ambiguous. When his student Joseph Weiss (in a 1947 article reproduced in *Briefe I*, pp. 458–60) argued that Scholem's esoteric method consisted of a form of "camouflage" in which the real person, "a secret metaphysician was disguised as an exact scientist," Scholem expressed his delight to Hugo Bergmann (letter 141, *Briefe I*, p. 332) about this "nice and cheeky essay" and approvingly noted that his pupils "had learned something from him." On the other hand, he was infuriated by Zwi Werblowsky's claim, concerning his inner motivation, that "the contemplative-scientific value of working on Sabbatianism compensates for the value of practicing strange acts." "I find myself," Scholem wrote, "confronted here with a phenomenon that is completely foreign to me: namely, this psychological interpretation into the reasons determining the relationship between a researcher and his field of study." See Scholem's letter to Werblowsky, January 13, 1958, reproduced in Skinner, *Gershom Scholem*, p. 329.
41. *Tagebücher 1*, p. 363, entry for August 14, 1916.
42. Ibid., pp. 448–49, entry for December 18, 1916.
43. In his moving condolence note to Fania Scholem (February 24, 1982), Hans Jonas wrote of her husband that "he was the focal

point, the center was where *he* was, the mover . . . an Urphänomen to use Goethe's word." See Scholem, *Briefe III,* p. 462.

44. Letter of Reinhold Scholem in Scholem, *Briefe III,* pp. 275–77, note to letter 26, February 29, 1972. The passage quoted appears on p. 275.

45. Ibid., pp. 28–29, letter 26, May 29, 1972.

46. *Tagebücher 1,* pp. 9–10.

47. Letter 34 to Werner Kraft, August 11, 1917, *Briefe 1,* p. 94.

48. *Tagebücher 1,* p. 53, entry for November 17, 1914.

49. Ibid., pp. 207–208, entry for December 18, 1915.

50. These notes, "Aufzeichnungen von Mutter," were made by Betty Scholem at Scholem's request when she visited Jerusalem in early 1931. See the "Anhang" (appendix) in Betty Scholem, Gershom Scholem, *Mutter und Sohn im Briefwechsel 1917–1946* (Munich: C. H. Beck, 1989), p. 531. I thank Antony Skinner for drawing my attention to this episode.

51. Scholem defined himself not as a "scientific" Marxist but as a "utopian socialist," "national" in character. He declined joining the German Social Democratic Party (unlike his brother, Werner) because, as he put it in his diary (January 5, 1916, *Tagebücher 1,* p. 229): "I do not want to represent the interests of a nation that I feel I have no right to represent and from whom I regard separation as an essential part of my task." He approvingly quoted Werner (July 29, 1916, ibid., p. 343), "when he wrote, it is not our task to prepare 'handkerchiefs for snotty German noses' ('deutsche Rotznasen'), for that is the role of the socialist movement."

52. The question was put by Werner Kraft. See Scholem's letter to him, letter 49, December 28, 1917, *Briefe 1,* p. 135. Note 9, p. 373, informs us that Heinle was indeed not Jewish.

53. *Tagebücher 1,* pp. 210–11, entry for December 21, 1915.

54. Letter 32, August 6, 1917, *Briefe I,* p. 90.

55. *Tagebücher 1,* p. 434, entry for November 24, 1916.

56. Ibid., p. 402, entry for October 11, 1916.

57. Scholem, to be sure, did occasionally make concessions in the other direction. Thus his comment to Theodor Adorno (letter 113 of June 4, 1939), in the context of the links between Kabbalah and neo-Platonism and gnosticism, that it was remarkable "how much the most original products of Jewish thinking are of a so-called assimilatory nature" (*Briefe I,* p. 275).

58. On this see Alter's excellent exposition in *Necessary Angels,* especially chapters 3 and 4.

59. Wasserstrom, *Religion after Religion.*

60. "Kabbalah and Myth" was the first lecture Scholem gave at

the Eranos society in Ascona (Switzerland). Eranos was a group of scholars committed to what Wasserstrom has described as a kind of redemptive project. Behind the camouflage of academic scholarship, he argues, these practitioners of a paradigmatic "History of Religions" sought to create an esoteric, postmonotheistic, nonlegalistic "religion after religion." The lecture is reproduced in Scholem's *On the Kabbalah and Its Symbolism*, trans. Ralph Manheim (New York: Schocken Books, 1969), pp. 87–117. The passage quoted appears on p. 117.

61. Letter 136 to Karl Löwith, August 31, 1968, *Briefe II*, p. 214.

62. Lichtheim to Scholem, letter 108a, November 28, 1966, and Scholem's brief remark that he had not suggested otherwise in letter 108 to Lichtheim, December 4, 1966, in Scholem, *Briefe II*, pp. 159, 162.

63. A study of the relationship and correspondence between Scholem and Lichtheim would make for interesting reading. See letters 40, 40a, 108, 108a, 109, 123, 126, 129, 129a, and 137 in *Briefe II*; letters 38, 42, 43, 52, 56 in *Briefe III*.

64. *Tagebücher 1*, p. 85, entry for January 27, 1915.

65. This "Laienpredigt" is reproduced in *Tagebücher 1*, pp. 297–98.

66. Letter 97 to Edith Rosenzweig, November 20, 1930, *Briefe I*, pp. 243–44.

67. *Tagebücher 1*, p. 226, entry for January 4, 1916.

68. Ibid., pp. 236–37, entry for January 10, 1916.

69. Thus his letter to his brother Werner, who he assumes will be surprised to hear from him: "Mommy's boy! Fanatic Jew! Horrible . . ." Letter 2, September 7, 1914, *Briefe I*, p. 3.

70. *Tagebücher 1*, p. 339, entry for July 23, 1916.

71. Ibid., p. 19, entry for March 5, 1913.

72. Ibid., p. 64, entry for November 27, 1914.

73. Ibid., p. 327, entry for June 28, 1916.

74. Werner was murdered by the Nazis in July 1940. See *Briefe I*, letters 2, 3, 4, and 5.

75. Ibid., p. 17, letter 17, October 9, 1916. "Hasidic words," Scholem added, "have a soul and in some way this soul is bound to the *magic form of the language*."

76. *Tagebücher 1*, p. 429, entry for November 21, 1916.

77. Ibid., pp. 430–31, entry for November 22, 1916.

78. Ibid., p. 339, entry for July 23, 1916.

79. Letter 63 to Aniela Jaffé, May 7, 1963, *Briefe II*, p. 95. I have used here the translation by Werner Brandl that appears in Wasserstrom, *Religion after Religion*, p. 189.

80. Letter 19 to Harry Heymann, November 12, 1916, *Briefe I*, p. 58.

81. *Tagebücher 1*, p. 360, entry for August 14, 1916. Scholem was careful to insert the religious dimension into this conception. In this light he declared (ibid., p. 403, entry for October 11, 1916), "And I know that *Zion is the absolute truth.* . . . *Zion is the measure of all things*" (italics his).

82. Ibid., p. 82, entry for January 20, 1915.

83. Though by March 23, 1915 (ibid., pp. 91–92) (incidentally, prior to his meeting with Walter Benjamin), he notes that he has rejected many points of Buber's Zionist doctrine. Those retained are what he calls its "destructive" aspects—the "constructive" ones he has put aside. On May 15, 1915 (ibid., p. 107), he wonders if Buber's writings—and attraction—can be seen as a form of "Rassenmystik." This distancing was, however, a gradual process. On May 22, 1915 (ibid., p. 117), Scholem still praises Buber—as opposed to Herzl—for not thinking in practical terms of colonization but rather in terms of the spiritual dimension, the soul of the Jewish people. He also notes (ibid., p. 119) Buber's influence on his perception of East European Jews: "And he found something immense. Overwhelming! He found beauty and reality, religiosity and unity in his Volk, the despised, pitied and supported Jews of the East. He discovered Hasidism again out of the rubble of a century, he found the chain of mysticism and the national myth that proceeds from the youth through the Volk, and he wrote down the myth not only as he discovered it, no, as he discovered it in himself. . . . and above all that occurs, in soft beauty, the myth lights the sun of his longing." However, see the very critical remarks on December 24, 1915 (ibid., p. 213), and the even longer ones on August 23, 1916 (ibid., pp. 387–88).

84. Letter 6 to Julie Schächter, August 29, 1915, *Briefe I*, p. 17.

85. *Tagebücher 1*, p. 83, entry for January 23, 1916.

86. Steiner, *Errata*, p. 10. I say "virtually" because Steiner writes that his own father had similar premonitions.

87. This, in spite of the fact that Scholem clearly followed the literature. See letter 78, which he wrote to George L. Mosse on January 12, 1965, commenting on the latter's *The Crisis of German Ideology* (*Briefe II*, pp. 121–22).

88. See the first and last chapters of my *Culture and Catastrophe* and my piece "On Saul Friedlander," *History and Memory* 9, nos. 1/2 (Fall 1997), for a consideration of an historian most sensitive to the (ongoing) nature of the issues.

89. One is tempted to say both Zionist and traditional-Jewish! How much irony was there in Scholem's question to Shalom Spiegel in 1939: "And what's happening with you? Are you sitting and discussing the horrible events in Germany and speculating about the allusions to

Hitler in the Book of Daniel . . . ?" Certainly this placed these events within a familiar frame, a known tradition. See letter 110, January 1, 1939, *Briefe I*, p. 269.

90. See Scholem's letter, number 106, to Benjamin, March 25, 1938, in *Correspondence of Walter Benjamin and Gershom Scholem*, pp. 214–15. The passage quoted appears on p. 215.

91. I am grateful to Anthony Skinner for pointing this out to me in conversation (in Jerusalem, August 4, 1999).

92. Letter 183, Scholem to his mother, April 20, 1933, *Briefwechsel 1917–1946*, pp. 294–95.

93. Ibid., p. 297, letter 185, April 26, 1933. Instead of then proceeding to analyze conditions in Nazi Germany, Scholem goes on to discuss how deeply the perspective on the Jewish Question has changed in Palestine and how the great majority of local *Ostjuden* perceive the German Jews as foreign and see more Germanness than Jewishness in them.

94. Ibid., p. 411, letter 250, March 7, 1936.

95. See his letter to Ulrich Gerhardt, May 3, 1933, *Briefe I*, p. 252.

96. See the entry for December 7, 1930, in his *Leben sammeln, nicht fragen wozu und warum*, vol. 1, *Tagebücher 1925–1932*, ed. Walter Nowojski and Christian Löser (Berlin: Aufbau-Verlag, 1996), p. 672.

97. *Religion after Religion*, pp. 190–91.

98. Ibid., p. 253. Scholem also declared that Jewish assimilation apart, another difference from 1492 lay in the desire of the persecutor to horribly humiliate the victim.

99. Thus his letter, number 18, to Walter Benjamin, April 13, 1933, in *Correspondence of Walter Benjamin and Gershom Scholem*, pp. 38–39. (The passage quoted appears on p. 39.)

100. The contents of this February 1940 letter can be found in Scholem's *Walter Benjamin: The Story of a Friendship*, pp. 222–24. The passage quoted can be found on p. 223.

101. The exchange between Scholem and Arendt first appeared in *Encounter* (January 1964).

102. Letter 131 of January 28, 1946, in *Briefe I*, pp. 309–14. The relevant passage of this important letter can be found on p. 312. It is worth quoting at length: "I know . . . that the Transfer problem was a great moral dilemma. You should actually also know that the only ones who, because they carried no responsibility for it, could please themselves with declamatory denunciations of transfer politics were the Revisionists! I believe that in the meantime experience has demonstrated that in the same situation each one of us would have dealt as the Zionist Organisation did, and that the only thing to be regretted is that

in a depraved world not more and emphatic use of this singular possibility was made to rescue Jews out of the hands of Fascism in time. You should know—and if you do not know, it should be said to you with great emphasis—that in the war we were prepared to buy Jews from the Gestapo and in that way large sums of good and hard money of the Joint [American Jewish Joint Distribution Committee] and the Zionists flowed into Germany, and that the people who conducted this thorny undertaking were not, as your logic would stamp them, betrayers of the Jewish people but rather people who did their duty. I would like to know that had Walter Benjamin's life depended upon it, we should not have saved him through such transactions! I must say that I credited you with more understanding for such a dialectic situation."

103. In his introduction to *Gershom Scholem: A Life in Letters*, p. 2, Antony Skinner comments upon Scholem's deeply committed stance and asks: "But if so, where was his moral voice during this time of such colossal destruction?"

104. See Scholem's letter, number 108, to George Lichtheim, December 4, 1966, in *Briefe II*, pp. 160–63. The relevant passage concerning his article on "Jews and Germans"—"about which I have had the opportunity for 40 years to reflect . . . and which is worked out in the text"—appears on p. 162.

105. Letter 137 of August 31, 1968, in *Briefe II*, pp. 213–14. The passage quoted appears on p. 214.

106. Robert Alter, "Modernism, the Germans and the Jews," *Commentary* 65, no. 3 (March 1978): 61–67.

107. See letter 178, *Briefe III*, pp. 193–94. See too the notes on p. 419.

108. See Peter Gay's "In Deutschland zu Hause," in *Die Juden im nationalsozialistichen Deutschland / The Jews in Nazi Germany, 1933–1943*, ed. Arnold Paucker (Tübingen: J. C. B. Mohr, 1986), p. 33.

2. HANNAH ARENDT AND THE COMPLEXITIES OF JEWISH SELFHOOD

1. See Robertson, *The 'Jewish Question' in German Literature*, pp. 362–66.

2. See Lawrence Baron, "Theodor Lessing: Between Jewish Self-Hatred and Zionism," *Leo Baeck Institute Yearbook* 26 (1981): 323–40.

3. The literature on Freud and Jung is legion. For the best account of the relationship in the present context, see Aldo Carotenuto, *A Secret Symmetry: Sabina Spielrein between Jung and Freud*, trans. Arno Pomerans, John Sheply, Krishna Winston (New York: Pantheon Books, 1982).

4. On the importance of Heinle to Benjamin, see Martin Jay,

"Against Consolation: Walter Benjamin and the Refusal to Mourn," in *War and Remembrance in the Twentieth Century*, ed. Jay Winter and Emanuel Sivan (New York: Cambridge University Press, 1999).

5. It is important to note that Scholem's communist brother, Werner, married the non-Jewish socialist, Emmy Wiechelt. The ironies here abound. Scholem's mother did not mind this union, but his father, "whose ideology ought to have made him welcome a mixed marriage," declined contact after a brief, formal meeting; and Scholem himself had "quite a good relationship with my sister-in-law." Scholem was amazed when, years later, she asked him why his brother had not insisted upon her joining the Jewish fold. "One year before her death she converted to Judaism because she wanted at least to be buried among Jews." Scholem was clearly aware, then, of some of the ironies and dynamics of these intimate relationships. See his *From Berlin to Jerusalem: Memories of My Youth*, trans. Harry Zohn (New York: Schocken Books, 1980), pp. 30–31. See too pp. 29–30 for his comments on other baptisms and intermarriages in his family.

6. Hannah Arendt, Kurt Blumenfeld, "*. . . in keinem Besitz verwurzelt.*" *Die Korrespondenz*, ed. Ingeborg Nordmann and Iris Pilling (Hamburg: Rotbuch Verlag, 1995).

7. Hannah Arendt, Hermann Broch, *Briefwechsel 1946–1951*, ed. Paul Michael Lützeler (Frankfurt am Main: Jüdischer Verlag, 1996).

8. *Between Friends: The Correspondence of Hannah Arendt and Mary McCarthy, 1949–1975*, ed. Carol Brightman (New York: Harcourt Brace, 1995).

9. *Hannah Arendt, Martin Heidegger, Briefe 1925–1975*, ed. Ursula Ludz (Frankfurt am Main: Vittorio Klostermann, 1998).

10. *Hannah Arendt, Karl Jaspers Correspondence, 1926–1969*, ed. Lotte Köhler and Hans Saner, translated from the German by Robert and Rita Kimber (New York: Harcourt Brace Jovanovich, 1992).

11. Arendt, Blücher, *Briefe 1936–1968*.

12. The complete Scholem-Arendt letters are due to appear within the next year or two. In the meantime, a more or less representative sample of their exchange has already appeared in the three-volume edition of Scholem's letters discussed extensively in chapter 1.

13. Arendt, letter 53 to Broch, July 26, 1950, *Briefwechsel*, p. 145. Scholem, incidentally, was also very critical of Koestler. See his letter to Arendt, number 129, August 6, 1945, *Briefe I*, pp. 303–304.

14. Interestingly, Arendt had already enunciated this in one of her first altercations with Scholem. After a heated exchange, she wrote to him: "I was not in the least offended by your letter but do not know how you will relate to mine. Ultimately you are *masculini generis* and thus naturally (perhaps) more vulnerable. Believe me, despite this let-

ter, for God's sake, I am not an honesty-fanatic. For me human relationships are far more important than so-called 'open exchanges.' . . . there is more worth in a person than in his opinions, on the simple ground that people de facto are more than what they think or do." Letter to Scholem, April 21, 1946, quoted in note 17 (of letter 131) in Scholem, *Briefe I*, pp. 453–54.

15. "On Humanity in Dark Times: Thoughts about Lessing," in her *Men in Dark Times* (New York: Harcourt Brace Jovanovich, 1968).

16. In the very first letter we have that Heidegger wrote to Arendt, number 1, February 10, 1925, he declares: "I can and will not separate your faithful eyes, your dear shape (*Gestalt*) from your pure trust, the goodness and purity of your maiden-like being." After years of separation during the Nazi period, Jaspers wrote after seeing her face reproduced again: "How happy we are to have your pictures. They are truly you, instantly recognizable. The same brilliant gleam of your eyes, but also etched in your face the sufferings of which your youth had no inkling. From your letters I have known for a long time now that you have come through undiminished. That was obviously not easy, and in these pictures I can see that it wasn't. You are a prodigal human being." See Arendt, Jaspers, *Correspondence 1926–1969*, p. 134, letter 88, March 15, 1949. The Blücher-Arendt relationship, as the letters we shall quote clearly indicate, was characterized by a peculiarly passionate mix of these ingredients.

17. See Elzbieta Ettinger, *Hannah Arendt, Martin Heidegger* (New Haven and London: Yale University Press, 1995). This work is unsatisfactory, for there is no serious attempt to link the affair to broader intellectual and political questions, to examine its ramifications in either Arendt's or Heidegger's thought.

18. Letter 43 (1929), Arendt, Heidegger, *Briefe 1925–1975*, p. 66.

19. Letter 44 (September 30, [1929?]), ibid., p. 67. The letter is made even more painful since Arendt relates this incident—in relation to the German version of the Pinocchio story—to a memory of her mother's once pretending not to recognize her: "I still know quite precisely the blind shock with which I still called: but I am your child, I am Hannah.—It was exactly like that today."

20. Ibid., pp. 21–25, letter 11, "Schatten."

21. See Arendt's letters to Blücher of February 8, 1950, in *Briefe 1936–1968*, p. 208. On Elfride's stupidities, antisemitism, and jealousies, see further the letter of May 24, 1952, ibid., p. 274. Moreover, Arendt wrote as much directly to Elfride, to whom she said that she was of such a cast of mind that she made "a conversation almost impossible for what the other says is already characterized in advance (and pardon me) catalogued—Jewish, German, Chinese. . . . The ad

hominem argument is the ruin of all understanding." See the Arendt, Heidegger, *Briefe 1925–1975*, pp. 77–78, letter of February 10, 1950.

22. Letter 297, November 1, 1961, Arendt, Jaspers, *Correspondence, 1926–1969*, p. 457.

23. Arendt, Heidegger, *Briefe 1925–1975*, p. 198, letter 120, March 12, 1970.

24. Letter 161, July 26, 1974, ibid., p. 250.

25. Letter 3, February 27, 1925, ibid., p. 14.

26. Letter 19, June 14, 1925, ibid., pp. 34–35. There are many such examples. Letter 2, February 21, 1925 (ibid., pp. 12–13), for instance, is written in a similar vein and reflects on the uniqueness of love and its ability to mutually transform while still allowing one to remain true to one's self.

27. Letter 12, April 24, 1925, ibid., p. 26.

28. See Steiner's masterful analysis of the correspondence, "The Magician in Love," *Times Literary Supplement*, January 29, 1999, pp. 3–4.

29. The phrase is Seyla Benhabib's. See her excellent essay, "The Personal Is Not the Political," which she gave to me after the lectures on which this book is based had been prepared; the essay appeared in *Boston Review*, October/November 1999, pp. 45–48.

30. "What Is Existential Philosophy?" reproduced in Hannah Arendt, *Essays in Understanding: 1930–1954*, ed. Jerome Kohn (New York: Harcourt Brace and Company, 1994), pp. 163–87.

31. Letter of January 3, 1950, Arendt, Blücher, *Briefe 1936–1968*, p. 190.

32. "Heidegger the Fox" is reproduced in Arendt, *Essays in Understanding*, pp. 361–62.

33. Letter to Blücher, June 20, 1952, Arendt, Blücher, *Briefe 1936–1968*, p. 293.

34. On this topic see the various analyses in Alan Milchman and Alan Rosenberg, eds., *Martin Heidegger and the Holocaust* (Atlantic Highlands, N.J.: Humanities Press, 1996).

35. Letter to Blücher from Paris, April 11, 1952, Arendt, Blücher, *Briefe 1936–1968*, p. 243.

36. "Herbert Marcuse and Martin Heidegger: An Exchange of Letters," *New German Critique* 53 (Spring/Summer 1991): 28–32.

37. For a good presentation of positions in the *Historikerstreit*, see Peter Baldwin, ed., *Reworking the Past: Hitler, the Holocaust, and the Historians' Debate* (Boston: Beacon Press, 1990), and my "History, Politics and National Memory: The German *Historikerstreit*," in *Survey of Jewish Affairs* 1988, ed. William Frankel (London: Associated University Presses, 1989).

38. Saul Friedlander correctly points out that classical "totalitar-

ian" approaches, while employing an essentially comparative method, did not entail relativization, because their tacit assumption *"ultimately maintained the Nazi case as the ne plus ultra, in relation to which other crimes were measured"* (italics his). The Nazi case was defined not by its "normal" but its catastrophic dimensions. See Saul Friedlander, "A Conflict of Memories? The New German Debates about the 'Final Solution,'" *Leo Baeck Memorial Lecture* 31 (New York: Leo Baeck Institute, 1987), pp. 9–10.

39. See "What Remains? The Language Remains: A Conversation with Günter Gaus," *Essays in Understanding*, p. 14.

40. Arendt, Blumenfeld, *". . . in keinem Besitz verwurzelt,"* p. 43, letter of July 19, 1947.

41. Alfred Kazin, *New York Jew* (New York: Knopf, 1978), p. 298.

42. See "Nazism, Culture and *The Origins of Totalitarianism:* Hannah Arendt and the Discourse of Evil," *New German Critique* 70 (Winter 1997): 117–39. See, too, my "Post-Holocaust Jewish Mirrorings of Germany: Hannah Arendt and Daniel Goldhagen," *Tel Aviv Jahrbuch für Deutsche Geschichte* 17 (1997): 345–53. Both these pieces are reproduced in my *In Times of Crisis: Essays on European Culture, Germans, and Jews* (Madison: University of Wisconsin Press, 2001).

43. See her "Approaches to the 'German Problem,'" *Essays in Understanding*, p. 111. The essay was first published in *Partisan Review* 13.1 (Winter 1945).

44. Ernst Gellner, "From Königsberg to Manhattan (Or Hannah, Rahel, Martin and Elfride or Thy Neighbour's Gemeinschaft)," *Culture, Identity and Politics* (Cambridge: Cambridge University Press, 1987). Arendt's depiction of totalitarianism, Gellner observes, "is itself very much in the romantic tradition even if here ironically, it is used to exculpate romanticism and philosophy from having fathered the allegedly alien evil" (p. 85). Here I will address the differences with Heidegger; but it also needs to be pointed out that Arendt—her, at times, rather overblown, ecstatic style notwithstanding—in various places also heavily criticized German romanticism. Although (as indicated above) I disagree with the main thrust of Gellner's argument, much of it is shrewd and incisive. Thus, he comments that Arendt's phenomenological method had no value when "extended to a new phenomenon and a new idea such as totalitarianism. . . . It then has a kind of inherent arbitrariness: whatever you put into the bag, you can also pull out" (pp. 89–90).

45. Richard Wolin, "Hannah and the Magician: An Affair to Remember," *New Republic*, October 9, 1995, pp. 27–37.

46. Like Heidegger, the Arendtian world revolves around ultimate existentialist moments. Her writings are not concerned with the quo-

tidian but rather with the totalitarian abyss or the ecstasy of the revolutionary moment, or with disinterested, virtuoso decision-making in the polis. See the insightful comment by George Kateb, "The Questionable Influence of Arendt (and Strauss)," in *Hannah Arendt and Leo Strauss: German Emigres and American Political Thought after World War II*, ed. P. G. Kielmansegg (Cambridge: Cambridge University Press, 1995).

47. See the interesting analysis by Leon Bramson, *The Political Context of Sociology* (Princeton: Princeton University Press, 1961).

48. The basic text for these themes is Dana R. Villa, *Arendt and Heidegger: The Fate of the Political* (Princeton: Princeton University Press, 1996).

49. Scholem, if the following anecdote is to be believed, harbored an active (and harmful) dislike for children. Upon a chance meeting in the street, Ernst Simon once introduced the six- or seven-year-old grandson of a distinguished Jerusalem judge to Scholem, who looked piercingly at the child and loudly declared: "I hate children." (This story was related to me by the insulted party himself, who has requested that he remain anonymous.)

50. Klemperer is the one exception to this, and even here I have thus far come across only a single reference to this issue (amongst the thousands of pages he wrote). In his diary entry for November 22, 1923, he writes: "I do not know if I should be happy or ill that we have no family additions. One is freer and lonelier. . . . I do not know if I have the heart to be a father." Compared to his friends and acquaintances, Klemperer complains, "it is painful to see how numb my heart is. Very numb and blunt and skeptical. It is a diminution of vitality . . . that I always see in front of my eyes." See *Leben sammeln, nicht fragen wozu und warum*, vol. 1, *Tagebücher 1918–1924*, p. 760.

51. Arendt, Heidegger, *Briefe 1925–1975*, pp. 68–69, letter 45, winter 1932/33.

52. This important letter is number 57, dated April 12, 1950; see ibid., pp. 93–95. The passage quoted appears on p. 94.

53. Letter 48, February 9, 1950, ibid., pp. 75–76. Later, Heidegger titled one of the poems he wrote for Arendt "Das Mädchen aus der Fremde."

54. See the Heidegger, Jaspers correspondence, *Briefwechsel 1920–1963*. The Heidegger-Jaspers (and Arendt) relationship is well analyzed in a two-piece article written by Mark Lilla after the Efroymson Lectures were given. See his "Ménage à Trois," in *The New York Review of Books*, November 18 and December 2, 1999, pp. 35–38 and pp. 25–29. The relationship is also briefly but well analyzed in Steiner, "The Magician in Love."

55. Arendt, Heidegger, *Briefe 1925–1975*, p. 110, letter 64, May 16, 1950.

56. See the analysis of the relationship in "Hannah Arendt and Karl Jaspers: Friendship, Catastrophe and the Possibilities of the German-Jewish Dialogue," in my *Culture and Catastrophe*.

57. Lilla, "Ménage à Trois" (November 18, 1999, p. 36), well analyzes Jaspers's awareness that the younger Heidegger was the superior thinker, that, indeed, Heidegger had seen through him and understood "what I failed to achieve." He also graphically documents Jaspers's gradual disillusion with Heidegger, the realization (December 2, 1999, p. 26) that Heidegger was demonic, "irredeemable—as a man and a thinker."

58. See her "What Is Existential Philosophy?" pp. 163–87. Anson Rabinbach has analyzed this comparison well in his "The German as Pariah: Karl Jaspers' *The Question of German Guilt*" in his *In the Shadow of Catastrophe: German Intellectuals between Apocalypse and Enlightenment* (Berkeley: University of California Press, 1997). See especially p. 152. See, too, in the same volume Rabinbach's perceptive essay, "Heidegger's 'Letter on Humanism' as Text and Event."

59. See the 1946 essay, "What Is Existential Philosophy?" The passage quoted appears on pp. 181–82.

60. This being said, we must add that it was also Heidegger's concept of "world," of existence as being-in-the-world, that Arendt regarded as a kind of immanent "step out of this difficulty" and which she would integrate into her political theory. See her 1954 speech to the American Society of Political Scientists, "Concern with Politics in Recent European Philosophical Thought," in *Essays in Understanding*, p. 443. See, on this, Jeffrey Andrew Barash, "The Political Dimension of the Public World: On Hannah Arendt's Interpretation of Martin Heidegger," in Larry May and Jerome Kohn, *On Hannah Arendt: Twenty Years Later* (Cambridge, Mass.: MIT Press, 1996), pp. 251–68. However, Barash, too, emphasizes Arendt's dissensions, rather than her borrowings, from Heidegger.

61. See ". . . *in keinem Besitz verwurzelt*," pp. 196–97, letter 78, December 16, 1957. Clearly, the admiration and the criticism often went together.

62. This was published in English as *The Question of German Guilt*, trans. E. B. Ashton (New York: Dial Press, 1947).

63. All this does not mean, of course, that there are no problems in Jaspers. For a discussion of the pertinent questions, see Rabinbach, "The German as Pariah."

64. This did not change over the years. In the wake of the 1967

war she wrote to Mary McCarthy: "But I know that any real catastrophe in Israel would affect me more deeply than almost anything else." Characteristically, though, she did preface this comment by criticizing the notion that while "empires, governments, nations come and go, the Jewish people remains. There is something grand and ignoble in this passion; I think I don't share it" (letter of October 17, 1969, *Between Friends*, p. 249).

65. Arendt, Jaspers, *Correspondence, 1926–1969*, p. 70, letter 50, December 17, 1946.

66. See "On Humanity in Dark Times," in *Men in Dark Times*, pp. 17–18, 23.

67. "What Remains?" p. 14.

68. Arendt, Jaspers, *Correspondence, 1926–1969*, pp. 18–19, letter 24, January 6, 1933.

69. Letter 22, January 1, 1933, ibid., p. 16.

70. Letter 23, January 3, 1933, ibid., pp. 17–18.

71. Letter 138, December 29, 1952, ibid., p. 204.

72. This was originally published in English. The most recent, and first complete edition, has just appeared. See Hannah Arendt, *Rahel Varnhagen: The Life of a Jewess*, ed. Liliane Weissberg (Baltimore: Johns Hopkins University Press, 1997).

73. See, for instance, *The Origins of Totalitarianism* (Cleveland and New York: World Publishing Company, 1951), pp. 66, 84–87. These notions were also very much part of the essays contained in *Men in Dark Times*.

74. Arendt, Jaspers, *Correspondence, 1926–1969*, pp. 204–205, letter 138, December 29, 1952.

75. For the full version of this remarkable text (which I have rather brutally amputated here) see letter 135, September 7, 1952, ibid., pp. 196–201.

76. Ibid.

77. Letter 43, August 17, 1946, ibid., p. 54. See the entire letter on pp. 51–56.

78. Letter 46, October 19, 1946, ibid., pp. 60–63. The passage quoted appears on p. 62.

79. Arendt accepted the view that all mythologization was undesirable but insisted that the economically useless nature of the murders rendered it unique. She was then struggling to formulate a notion of "radical evil" commensurate with the horrors of the corpse-factories. See letter 60, December 17, 1946, ibid., pp. 68–70. For an analysis of this discussion, see "Hannah Arendt and Karl Jaspers," in my *Culture and Catastrophe*.

80. See Arendt's "Karl Jaspers: A Laudatio," in *Men in Dark Times,* pp. 71–80.

81. Arendt, Jaspers, *Correspondence, 1926–1969,* p. 404, letter 267, October 14, 1960.

82. "On Humanity in Dark Times," especially pp. 26–31.

83. Letter to Gershom Scholem, July 24, 1963, reprinted in Hannah Arendt, *The Jew as Pariah,* ed. Ron H. Feldman (New York: Grove Press, 1978), p. 247.

84. "On Humanity in Dark Times," p. 18.

85. Arendt, Jaspers, *Correspondence, 1926–1969,* p. 70, letter 50, December 17, 1946.

86. Ibid.

87. See Elisabeth Young-Bruehl, *Hannah Arendt: For Love of the World* (New Haven and London: Yale University Press, 1982), p. 127. Unfortunately, Young-Bruehl provides no explanation for this extraordinary step.

88. Arendt, Jaspers, *Correspondence, 1929–1969,* p. 29, letter 34, January 29, 1946.

89. Arendt, Blücher, *Briefe 1936–1968,* p. 45, letter of August 12, 1936.

90. Arendt herself had expressed concern about contemporary "eagerness to see recorded, displayed and discussed in public what were once strictly private affairs and nobody's business." See Benhabib, "The Personal Is Not the Political," p. 45. Arendt's objection could possibly be less valid with regard to Heidegger given the "public" dimensions and political implications of this affair and the influence the relationship might have had on her thought (though the nitty-gritty details would also certainly be irrelevant here). With regard to Blücher, however, such passages do indeed appear to conform to the realm of the utterly private. It is worth noting, however, that when I expressed my puzzlement about the publication of some of the highly erotic Arendt-Blücher letters and wondered whether or not Arendt would have approved of reproducing them, Lotte Köhler, editor of the correspondence and a lifelong friend of the philosopher, responded crisply: "Well, she did not burn those letters!"

91. Letter of February 21, 1937, Arendt, Blücher, *Briefe 1936–1968,* p. 71. The letter ends: "I kiss you all over. . . . within you; I want to be in your arms again, between the legs, on the mouth, on the breast, in the womb of my woman." His letter of February 22, 1937 (ibid., p. 72) reads: "I want that you give yourself totally and boundlessly, I want you to open all the locks; let the beautiful, strong torrent of your love fill me up; yes I swim in it, it carries me, it moves

me forward. Let yourself go entirely, have no feminine anxiety, be *my* woman." And Arendt in her reply (February 23, 1937, ibid., p. 74) declares: "Dear, dearest Heinrich, my one and everything, mine completely—I can no longer write for all I can do is think that I will have you tomorrow, with me and in me."

92. Ibid. See the letters of Blücher, September 15, 1937, and Arendt, September 16, 1937, ibid., pp. 82–83. See, too, Arendt's great declaration of love (September 18, 1937, ibid., pp. 83–84), her discovery that one did not have to fear that love meant losing oneself (probably an oblique reference to Heidegger).

93. See the letters of December 14, 1949, and March 30, 1952, ibid., pp. 175 and 237, respectively. That Arendt also employed many Yiddishisms in her letters to Broch is, of course, less surprising.

94. Letter of August 24, 1936, ibid., pp. 57–58.

95. Letter of August 8, 1936, ibid., p. 39.

96. These are most conveniently found in Arendt, *The Jew as Pariah.*

97. See especially chapter 2 of Michael Walzer, *Interpretation and Social Criticism* (Cambridge, Mass.: Harvard University Press, 1987).

98. See Scholem's letter (119) to Shalom Spiegel, July 17, 1941, in Gershom Scholem, *Briefe I,* p. 285.

99. Letter of July 24, 1963, pp. 246–47 in *The Jew as Pariah.*

100. See letter 49, November 28, 1955, in Arendt, Blumenfeld, *". . . in keinem Besitz verwurzelt,"* pp. 135–36. The second part of this comment is a little strange. Now that the correspondence with Blücher has been published (one can only guess at the content of their casual conversations!), there is very little evidence that Arendt shied away from too many critical comments about the Jews in Blücher's presence.

101. I examine the entire complex of Arendt's relationship to Scholem, Jewishness, Israel, and Zionism in my essay "Hannah Arendt in Jerusalem," which will be published in a book of the same title that I am editing for the University of California Press (2001).

102. Letter 133 to Hans Paeschke, March 24, 1968, Scholem, *Briefe II,* p. 210.

103. As it does for the person they both deeply admired, Walter Benjamin.

104. David Suchoff, "Gershom Scholem, Hannah Arendt, and the Scandal of Jewish Particularity," *Germanic Review* 72, no. 1 (Winter 1997): 57–76. The quoted material appears on pp. 57–58. I thank Paul Mendes-Flohr for drawing my attention to this essay.

105. For Scholem's attitude, see letter 133, *Briefe II,* pp. 209–10.

106. Letter 65 to Kurt Blumenfeld, January 9, 1957, in Arendt, Blumenfeld, *". . . in keinem Besitz verwurzelt,"* pp. 174–77. The passage

quoted appears on p. 176. When Arendt remarked that Scholem had no ears she meant, of course, that he did not listen. Anyone who knew Scholem or has seen a picture of him will know how prominent a feature of his anatomy his ears were!

107. For her appreciation of the extraordinary nature of that experience ("nothing comparable to it is to be found even in the other areas of Jewish assimilation") and the challenge of historically understanding it, see her preface to *Rahel Varnhagen*, p. xvii.

108. Although it is interesting to note that Arendt perceived Scholem exactly within this light: "Benjamin's choice, baroque in a double sense, has an exact counterpart in Scholem's strange decision to approach Judaism via the Cabala, that is, that part of Hebrew literature which is untransmitted and untransmissible in terms of Jewish tradition, in which it has always had the odor of something downright disreputable. Nothing showed more clearly—so one is inclined to say today—that there was no such thing as a 'return' to either the German or the European or the Jewish tradition than the choice of these fields of study. It was an implicit admission that the past spoke directly only through these things that had not been handed down, whose seeming closeness to the present was thus due precisely to their exotic character, which ruled out all claims to a binding authority." See Arendt's essay "Walter Benjamin: 1892–1940," in *Men in Dark Times*, p. 195.

109. Ibid., p. 190.

110. "... *in keinem Besitz verwurzelt,*" letter 19, October 14, 1952, p. 68.

3. Victor Klemperer and the Shock of Multiple Identities

1. Hannah Arendt, *Men in Dark Times* (New York: Harcourt Brace Jovanovich, 1968).

2. I have carefully combed her works and biography and, to date, have come across no mention of him. Nor have I thus far come across any mention of Arendt or Scholem in Klemperer. This may be partly explained by the age differences. Klemperer was born in 1881, Scholem in 1897, and Arendt in 1906.

3. Victor Klemperer, *LTI; Notizbuch eines Philologen* (Berlin: Aufbau-Verlag, 1947).

4. A less charitable view holds that the Latin term *lingua tertii imperii* was not a coded term used out of fear of the Nazis but rather a form of *bildungs* snobbism, an example of a professor wanting to flaunt his knowledge of Latin. See the review of the diaries by Eva Auf der Maur in *Freiburger Rundbrief. Zeitschrift für christlich-jüdische Begegnung* 6, no. 4 (1999): 297–300, especially p. 298.

5. The connections between the analysis and the personal experience merit a separate study. For one instance, see his memoirs, *Curriculum Vitae. Erinnerungen 1881–1918* (Berlin: Aufbau-Verlag, 1996), vol. 1, pp. 280–81.

6. George Steiner, the person most responsible for popularizing the issue of language and barbarism, for instance, first published his musings on the topic without even having heard of the book. See his starred note to the essay "The Hollow Miracle," in *Language and Silence: Essays on Language, Literature, and the Inhuman* (New York: Atheneum, 1977), p. 95. The essay was originally written in 1959. Those interested in the field had heard of Klemperer, but few had actually read him.

7. The first volume appeared in English with the title *I Shall Bear Witness: The Diaries of Victor Klemperer, 1933–41*, abridged and translated by Martin Chalmers (London: Weidenfeld & Nicolson, 1998). The second volume, *I Shall Bear Witness: The Diaries of Victor Klemperer, 1942–45* (London: Weidenfeld & Nicolson, 1999) appeared after this manuscript had been prepared for publication. I have thus used volume 2 of the German edition for the years 1942 to 1945; see Victor Klemperer, *Ich will Zeugnis ablegen bis zum letzten: Tagebücher 1933–1945*, 2 vols. (Berlin: Aufbau-Verlag, 1995), ed. Walter Nowojski with the assistance of Hadwig Klemperer.

8. See the massive two-volume diaries covering the turbulent years of the Weimar Republic (1918–24; 1925–32): Victor Klemperer, *Leben sammeln, nicht fragen wozu und warum* (Berlin: Aufbau-Verlag, 1996), ed. Walter Nowojski with the assistance of Christian Löser.

9. This said, there is little doubt that Klemperer's fame will continue to reside in his name as a great diarist rather than as a student of French literature, or even as an analyst of totalitarianism.

10. Though he is not yet sufficiently known in the English-speaking world, the publication of *I Shall Bear Witness* did receive much publicity as well as critical analysis and acclaim. Most prominently, see Peter Gay, "Inside the Third Reich," *New York Times Book Review*, November 22, 1998, pp. 15–16; Omer Bartov, "The Last German," *New Republic*, December 28, 1998, pp. 34–42. The publication of the diaries in German also attracted attention. See, for instance, Amos Elon, "The Jew Who Fought to Stay German," *New York Times Magazine*, March 24, 1996.

11. See Paolo Traverso's brilliant analysis not only of the reception but also of the diaries themselves: "Victor Klemperers Deutschlandbild—Ein jüdisches Tagebuch?" in *Deutschlandbilder, Tel Aviv Jahrbuch für Deutsche Geschichte* 26 (1997): 307–44.

12. See my "Reconceiving the Holocaust?" *Tikkun* 11, no. 4 (July–August 1996): 62–65, and "Archetypes and the German-Jewish Dialogue: Reflections Occasioned by the Goldhagen Affair," *German History* 15, no. 2 (1997): 240–50. Of particular interest in the present context may be my "Post-Holocaust Mirrorings of Germany: Hannah Arendt and Daniel Goldhagen," *Tel Aviv Jahrbuch für Deutsche Geschichte* 26 (1997): 345–53.

13. See the two-volume *So sitze ich denn zwischen allen Stühlen* (*Tagebücher* 1945–1949; 1950–1959), ed. Walter Nowojski with Christian Löser (Berlin: Aufbau-Verlag, 1999).

14. Victor Klemperer, *Curriculum Vitae. Erinnerungen 1881–1918*, 2 vols., ed. Walter Nowojski (Berlin: Aufbau-Verlag, 1996).

15. See the entry for December 3, 1938, *I Shall Bear Witness*, p. 266. Such examples can be multiplied many times over.

16. Ibid., p. 152, entry for April 5, 1936.

17. Ibid., p. 223, entry for August 6, 1937.

18. Ibid., p. 334, entry for July 24, 1940.

19. Ibid., p. 315, entry for March 17, 1940.

20. Ibid., p. 183, entry for September 27, 1936.

21. Ibid., p. 310, entry for New Year's Eve, 1939.

22. Thus as late as July 21, 1944, Klemperer wrote: "So wenig wissen wir im Judenhaus, was vorgeht." See *Ich will Zeugnis ablegen*, vol. 2, p. 549.

23. On Buchenwald, see the entries for November 25 and December 6, 1938, *I Shall Bear Witness*, pp. 261, 268. "When did I first hear the name Theresienstadt?" Klemperer asks on July 9, 1942 (*Ich will Zeugnis ablegen*, vol. 2, p. 160), and replies: "It must have been this winter" (ibid.); see too the entry for August 6, 1942 (ibid., p. 194), where he speaks of transportation to places like Theresienstadt as appearing to him and other Jews as "self-evident."

24. See the entry for October 25, 1941: "Even more shocking reports about deportations to Poland" (*I Shall Bear Witness*, p. 421).

25. Ibid., pp. 368–69, entry for May 21, 1941. See too the entry for August 22, 1941 (ibid., p. 408): "There is widespread talk now of the killing of the mentally ill in the asylums."

26. Ibid., p. 47, entry for March 16, 1942.

27. Ibid., p. 68, entry for April 19, 1942.

28. Ibid., p. 259, entry for October 17, 1942. Here Klemperer talks about two women deported to Auschwitz, "which appears to be a fast-working slaughterhouse."

29. Ibid. See for instance the entries for October 30, 1942 (p. 268), and August 14, 1944 (p. 561). On January 29, 1945 (ibid., p.

648), Klemperer is told of Thomas Mann's speech in which he declares that the Germans have murdered and gassed Jews in Auschwitz by the millions.

30. Ibid., p. 385, entry for May 29, 1943. The article appeared in the journal *Freiheitskampf.*

31. Ibid., p. 206, entry for August 14, 1942.

32. Ibid., p. 606, entry for October 24, 1944.

33. Anyone reading only the war diaries could easily gain the impression that the doubts, the complaints about health, and the pessimism were essentially a product of the Nazi years. This is definitely not so, as a cursory reading of the Weimar diaries indicates. There, too, it is a constantly recurring theme. The entry of June 15, 1919, for example, reads thus: "My mood sinks ever deeper. Without satisfaction, without respect for one's own work, without hope in the future. And always more lonely" (*Leben sammeln*, vol. 1, p. 126). See too the entry for June 17, 1919, ibid., p. 127. On March 7, 1920, Klemperer quotes Goethe to the effect that the healthy man does not think of death, then adds: "But then I am not a healthy man" (ibid., p. 244). Despite the achievements he lists for the year 1920, he sums up the year on December 31 as follows: "And still no feeling of happiness. I feel sick, aged, the future unknown" (ibid., p. 397).

34. Ibid. These qualities were always intertwined. As he put it on November 2, 1942: "And in me always the curiosity of the chronicler and the fear for my own fate" (ibid., p. 270).

35. *Curriculum Vitae*, vol. 1, p. 17.

36. Ibid., p. 42.

37. See Kafka's biting and bitter critique of the empty, hypocritical religious education he received in *Letter to his Father*, trans. Ernst Kaiser and Eithne Wilkins (New York: Schocken Books, 1953). The letter was originally written in November 1917.

38. *Curriculum Vitae*, vol. 1, p. 41.

39. Ibid., p. 109. On the interrelated disdain for Yiddish and elevation of High German among liberal, Enlightened, bourgeois German Jews, see my *Brothers and Strangers: The East European Jew in German and German-Jewish Consciousness, 1800–1923* (Madison: University of Wisconsin Press, 1982; paperback edition, 1999), especially pp. 8–11.

40. Ibid., p. 248.

41. On this as a more generalized phenomenon, see Sidney M. Bolkosky, *The Distorted Image: German Jewish Perceptions of Germans and Germany, 1918–1935* (New York: Elsevier, 1975). There is some validity to Bolkovsky's critical approach, but one would want to register certain reservations related to the wisdom of hindsight.

42. *Curriculum Vitae*, vol. 1, p. 287.

43. *Ich will Zeugnis ablegen,* vol. 2, p. 327, entry for February 7, 1943.
44. See the entry for October 6, 1936, *I Shall Bear Witness,* p. 129.
45. On this, see George L. Mosse, *German Jews beyond Judaism* (Bloomington: Indiana University Press and Cincinnati: Hebrew Union College Press, 1985), p. 15.
46. See "On Humanity in Dark Times: Thoughts about Lessing," in Arendt's *Men in Dark Times.*
47. Mosse, *German Jews beyond Judaism.*
48. Ibid., pp. 16–18.
49. *Leben sammeln,* vol. 1, p. 45, entry for January 3, 1919.
50. *Curriculum Vitae,* vol. 2, pp. 571–72.
51. See Robertson, *The 'Jewish Question' in German Literature,* p. 267.
52. Thus, typically, the diary entry for June 20, 1939: "Constant reading aloud: the 16th and for the time being final volume of *Jean Christophe.* At least I brush up my French and my relationship to modern French literature. In good moments I am once again playing with the possibility of a supplement to my 19th and 20th century" (*I Shall Bear Witness,* p. 289). The passion not just for recording but for study and work went on until the very end. See, for instance, the entry for August 30, 1944, *Ich will Zeugnis ablegen,* vol. 2, p. 572. These functions of work were clear to the very honest Klemperer: "Things are so bad," Klemperer wrote on November 29, 1942, of an acquaintance, "that I cannot feel compassion for the man, only the anxiety that the same fate awaits me. Arbeiten, mich in Arbeit betrinken!" (ibid., pp. 284–85).
53. *I Shall Bear Witness,* pp. 176–77, entry for August 16, 1936.
54. "If I could be a believer," Klemperer wrote on March 7, 1920, "I could only be a Catholic; Protestantism is a half measure, an attempt at a compromise where none can exist, not faith and not reason" (*Leben sammeln,* vol. 1, p. 245). It is noteworthy that Klemperer did not even think of Judaism here as a possible option.
55. This was a gradual process. Klemperer still spoke, relatively unself-consciously, of himself as a Protestant on October 9, 1936. See ibid., p. 186.
56. On this see Traverso, "Victor Klemperers Deutschlandbild," p. 341.
57. *Leben sammeln,* vol. 2, pp. 533–34, entry for June 28, 1929.
58. Martin Chalmers, the translator into English of *I Shall Bear Witness,* writes in his introduction that these ailments played another role: "At times, the couple seem bound together by their illnesses, real and imagined" (*I Shall Bear Witness,* p. xv). Perhaps, too, the couple's

almost obsessive concentration on domestic matters—the concern with their new car, their fixation on the details and troubles related to the building of a house—may similarly have functioned to deflect outward any emotions of *ressentiment*.

59. See *Ich will Zeugnis ablegen*, vol. 2, p. 338, the entry for March 2, 1943, where Klemperer comments on the protective function of mixed marriage.

60. All this information is culled from the invaluable study by Nathan Stoltzfus, *Resistance of the Heart: Intermarriage and the Rosenstrasse Protest in Nazi Germany* (New York: W. W. Norton, 1996).

61. Ibid., p. 306, note 70. The source is at the Berlin Document Center, File 0.240.11, and the material quoted is from as late as 1944.

62. Ibid., especially p. 102. This gender decision was taken, according to Stoltzfus, in order to prevent unrest by pacifying that segment of intermarried Jews most influential in German society.

63. See "Heroismus statt eines Vorwortes," in *LTI*, pp. 9–16.

64. *I Shall Bear Witness*, p. 21, entry for June 30, 1933.

65. Ibid., p. 431, entry for December 22, 1941.

66. Ibid., p. 183, entry for September 21, 1919. The diaries are replete with such incidents and reports of antisemitic sentiment. There is no way these can all be noted. See, for instance, the entry for February 12, 1919, in *Leben sammeln*, vol. 1, p. 68: "What luck for Europe that there are Jews. They are always responsible for war and peace, profit, damage, everything painful!" On November 7, 1923, he notes the rioting and plundering in the East European Jewish quarter in Berlin and the attempts to hush it up (ibid., p. 758). On the shameful attempt to prevent Jews from taking the baths at Zinnowitz, Klemperer notes in August 1927 that such agitation was allowed while any communist action was forbidden. See *Leben sammeln*, vol. 2, p. 369, entry for August 20, 1927.

67. The Weimar diaries are (sometimes wearingly) packed with the insecurities, jealousies, rivalries, and politics of German academic life in this period.

68. The antisemitism was often tied to political events (especially questions of French-German relations, on which Klemperer was an expert). See the entry for January 18, 1923, *Leben sammeln*, vol. 1, p. 654.

69. Klemperer's diaries not only faithfully report the anti-Jewish atmosphere of the times but also the critical remarks of other Jews aimed at him specifically as an "unappetizing" convert. See, for instance, the entries for April 8 and 17, 1919, *Leben sammeln*, vol. 1, pp. 94, 100.

70. Ibid., p. 184, September 21, 1919. See too the entry for January 24, 1918, ibid., p. 56.

71. Ibid., p. 401, January 5, 1921.

72. Ibid., pp. 480–81, entry for August 12, 1921.

73. See, for instance, the entry for October 29, 1929, *Leben sammeln,* vol. 2, p. 611.

74. Ibid., p. 361, entry for August 6, 1927.

75. "Im übrigen war es ein schöner jüdischer Abend" (entry for February 18, 1923, *Leben sammeln,* vol. 1, p. 661). Klemperer was quite aware that he tended to socialize in mainly Jewish circles. See ibid., p. 796, entry for March 10, 1924.

76. Ibid., pp. 305–306, entry for June 6, 1920.

77. *Leben sammeln,* vol. 2, p. 61, entry for May 26, 1925.

78. *Leben sammeln,* p. 537, entry for December 18, 1921. On September 20, 1922, Klemperer reports on an evening at which, with his guests, "wir viel gemauschelt haben [we talked much in a Jewish manner]" (ibid., p. 620).

79. More accurately, Scholem argued—more in the case of friendship than marriage—that in order for such intimacy to really occur, the Gentile had to turn into a very rare bird, "a Jewish non-Jew." See letter 49 to Werner Kraft, December 28, 1917, in Scholem, *Briefe I,* p. 135.

80. Ibid., p. 17, entry for March 13, 1925.

81. In his memoirs (written during the Nazi period), he states that while he cannot honor what the Germans are doing, Ernst Lissauer's "Hate Song against England" of 1914 was truly felt and authentic. See *Curriculum Vitae,* vol. 1, pp. 280–81. "We Germans were better than the others, freer in thought, purer in feelings, quieter and more just in commerce. We, we Germans were the really chosen people" (ibid., p. 315). Yet Klemperer was throughout somewhat torn, his thought and person too sophisticated for any one-dimensional position. Thus in a diary entry for April 20, 1921, he wrote: "And with this the split of my feelings: For me the Kaisertum is a flag, I long for the old German power, I would mightily like to strike France again. But what loathsome company one is with the Deutsch-Völkischen! They would be even more disgusting if Austria came to us. And everything that we feel now is ultimately what the French felt with more or less justification after 70 [i.e., 1870]. And under Wilhelm II, I did not become an Ordinarius. . . . The objective situation is as split as my subjective feeling" (*Leben sammeln,* vol. 1, pp. 433–34).

82. See the entry for December 30, 1918, *Leben sammeln,* vol. 1, p. 40.

83. See, for instance, the diary entry for July 30, 1936, where he comments of the *Economie politique* that "whole passages could be from Hitler's speeches"; and on July 19, 1937, he writes: "Rousseau has

never triumphed to such a degree nor been taken ad absurdum to such a degree as today. The posthumous unmasking of Rousseau is called Hitler" (*I Shall Bear Witness*, pp. 173, 221).

84. J. L. Talmon, *The Origins of Totalitarian Democracy* (London: Secker & Warburg, 1955), especially chapter 3.

85. See Traverso, "Victor Klemperers Deutschlandbild," pp. 317–18. This was more balanced, contextual analysis than simple praise. See too his diary entry for June 17, 1920, in which he calls Barres "Catholic, chauvinist" (*Leben sammeln*, vol. 1, p. 312).

86. For Klemperer's comments on this, see *Leben sammeln*, vol. 1, p. 179, the entry for September 16, 1919. See too the entry for March 14, 1920 (ibid., p. 245), where the conflict between his right-leaning tendencies and antisemitism is made very explicit. There, too, he complains of the difficulties of finding a decent political identity. The Left certainly was no option: "Who embodies the democratic, the German, the humane idea?" Yet his distaste for the radical antisemitic right was great enough that he could write on March 20, 1920, that "my sympathies are with no one: but if I have to choose, then better the Räterepublik than the Herrn, Lieutenants and Antisemites" (ibid., p. 250). Klemperer also expresses his distaste for a Jewish acquaintance, Leo Sternberg, who supported the Kapp putsch: "As Jew, judge, Rheinländer! Three impossibilities" (ibid., p. 250, March 21, 1920).

87. *I Shall Bear Witness*, entry for March 31, 1933, p. 10.

88. See, for instance, Victor Klemperer, *Romanische Sonderart. Geistesgeschichtliche Studien* (Munich, 1926). The notes he made in his diary while preparing this volume contain such notions as: "The German can live only in *becoming*, the *Roman* only in being" (see the entry for September 5, 1921, *Leben sammeln*, vol. 1, p. 497). On this see Traverso, "Victor Klemperers Deutschlandbild," p. 314. The matter is complicated, for together with a later suspicion of generalization, the conviction that collectives had their own characteristics persisted. On July 6, 1942, he asked: "What do we mean *the* Jews, *the* Germans, etc.? And yet group characters exist." See *Ich will Zeugnis ablegen*, vol. 2, p. 158. See too the entry for September 14, 1943, ibid., pp. 426–27.

89. *I Shall Bear Witness*, p. 7, entry for March 17, 1933.

90. Ibid., p. 11, entry for April 3, 1933; see *Ich will Zeugnis ablegen*, vol. 1, p. 18. The English version does not have the full citation. The translation is partly mine. On April 25, Klemperer repeats his disillusionment with national psychology but goes on to say in the next sentence: "Perhaps the current madness is indeed a typically German madness" (*I Shall Bear Witness*, pp. 14–15).

91. Ibid., p. 221, entry for July 19, 1937. And on January 11,

1938, he writes simply that "the whole national ideology has quite gone to pieces for me" (ibid., p. 237).

92. *I Shall Bear Witness*, pp. 260–61, entry for October 9, 1938.

93. Ibid., p. 23, entry for July 1, 1933.

94. Ibid., p. 123, entry for July 21, 1935.

95. Ibid., p. 305, entry for November 12, 1939.

96. *Ich will Zeugnis ablegen*, vol. 1, pp. 383–84, entry for October 27, 1937.

97. See *Leben sammeln*, vol. 2, p. 49, entry for April 27, 1925: "What will become of Germany? . . . freedom is no longer the keyword of youth but rather "Order." Fascism is everywhere. The shocks of the war are forgotten: the Russian terror is driving Europe into reaction. . . . Nationalism begets nationalism."

98. See *Leben sammeln*, p. 351, entry for September 3, 1920.

99. Ibid., p. 9, entry for March 30, 1933.

100. Ibid., p. 205, entry for March 27, 1937.

101. Ibid., p. 224, entry for August 17, 1937.

102. Ibid., p. 421, entry for October 25, 1941.

103. Ibid., p. 240, entry for February 23, 1938.

104. Ibid., p. 242, entry for April 5, 1938.

105. *Ich will Zeugnis ablegen*, vol. 2, pp. 140–41, entry for June 23, 1942. Given Klemperer's great sensitivity to political language, we might ask whether he was using these biological analogies ironically.

106. Ibid., p. 201, entry for August 10, 1942.

107. Ibid., p. 253, entry for August 24, 1938.

108. *Leben sammeln*, vol. 2, p. 643, entry for August 6, 1930.

109. *I Shall Bear Witness*, p. 60, entry for April 5, 1934. When speaking of loud and ill-mannered children, Klemperer would characterize their behavior as "out of the ghetto." See *Leben sammeln*, vol. 1, p. 402.

110. Ibid., p. 333, entry for July 18, 1940.

111. Ibid., p. 128, entry for October 6, 1935.

112. Ibid., p. 365, entry for April 16, 1941.

113. See, for example, the entry for September 5, 1944, ibid., p. 576.

114. *Ich will Zeugnis ablegen*, vol. 2, pp. 545–46, entries for July 17 and 19, 1944.

115. "Herzl is disagreeable to me but interesting. Buber's 'Chassidim,' his introduction to Jewish mysticism, makes me literally sick." Ibid., p. 145, entry for June 25, 1942. The diaries are dotted with other such negative remarks. His comments in *LTI*, pp. 233–34, are more positive.

116. *Ich will Zeugnis ablegen,* vol. 2, p. 133, entry for June 14, 1942.

117. Ibid., p. 88, entry for May 18, 1942.

118. On Elbogen's relationship to Otto Klemperer, see ibid., p. 19, the entry for June 17, 1933. Victor earlier described his relationship to Otto thus: "I have always felt something competitive with Otto Kl. We are the same, at present the youngest, generation, and we represent 'art.' Now he is high up [at the Berlin Staatsoper] and I feel myself oppressed" (*Leben sammeln,* vol. 1, p. 701, entry for June 8, 1923). Yet a little later (January 4, 1925), discussing Otto's contemporary fame and success, he made a prediction that was rather accurate but for reasons he surely could not have anticipated: "I say to myself, he is today famous for thousands and I am unknown. But, like an actor, one forgets a conductor after his death. And my book after 100 years will perhaps be read by 100 people. Vanitas vanitatum" (*Leben sammeln,* vol. 2, p. 7). Klemperer subsequently also documented how the Nazis exploited Otto's instability: "A report in the *Dresdener NN:* 'Yid' Klemperer who yiddified the Berlin Opera has escaped from the mental asylum in Hollywood and been caught again" (*I Shall Bear Witness,* p. 361, entry for March 4, 1941).

119. *Ich will Zeugnis ablegen,* vol. 2, p. 56, entry for March 27, 1942.

120. See the detailed description of this (and Klemperer's success as an itinerant lecturer on the Jewish literature circuit) in *Curriculum Vitae,* vol. 1, pp. 494–98. On Franzos and his ideological centrality for such liberal Jews, see my *Brothers and Strangers,* especially pp. 27–31. It was during this period, incidentally, that Scholem read Klemperer's articles on Arthur Schnitzler. See Scholem's *Tagebücher 1,* pp. 134–35, entry for July 25, 1915.

121. See the diary entry for June 29, 1923, where he writes that the Zionists "are not any more broad-minded [weitstirniger] than the people of the swastika" (*Leben sammeln,* vol. 1, p. 706).

122. These comments were made in the context of Klemperer's earlier reading of Gronemann's book, *Hawdoloh und Zapfenstreich,* concerning his World War I experiences on the Eastern Front and his discovery of the Eastern Jews there. See *Curriculum Vitae,* vol. 2, pp. 478–82. The material quoted appears on pp. 480–81.

123. *I Shall Bear Witness,* p. 22, entry for July 9, 1933.

124. Ibid., p. 113, entry for April 22, 1935: Zionism "I call . . . betrayal and Hitlerism." See the entry for October 18, 1936, ibid., p. 190.

125. Ibid., p. 66, entry for June 13, 1934.

126. *Ich will Zeugnis ablegen,* vol. 2, p. 49, entry for March 17, 1942.

127. Ibid., p. 77, entry for May 3, 1942.

128. Ibid., p. 348, entry for December 10, 1940.

129. Ibid., p. 146, entry for June 26, 1942.

130. Ibid., pp. 142, 144, entries for June 23, 1942, and June 25, 1942.

131. Ibid., p. 150, entry for July 1, 1942.

132. Ibid., pp. 13–14, entry for January 19, 1942.

133. *LTI,* pp. 228–32.

134. On Klemperer's understanding that, given the new political atmosphere, the "Zion" chapter could be reinserted, see the entry for January 19, 1953, in *So sitze ich denn zwischen allen Stühlen. Tagebücher 1950–1959,* ed. Walter Nowojski with Christian Löser (Berlin: Aufbau-Verlag, 1999), p. 353. On his delight, see the entry for January 24, 1953 (p. 354), where he comments: "At the same time triumph for my Zion chapter in LTI." On Merker, see volume 1 of *So sitze ich denn zwischen allen Stühlen. Tagebücher 1945–1949,* ed. Walter Nowojski with Christian Löser (Berlin: Aufbau-Verlag, 1999), entry for December 3, 1948, p. 611; and in vol. 2, see the entries for September 3, 1950, pp. 79–80; October 16, 1950, p. 97; February 22, 1953, p. 360; and March 2, 1953, p. 363. Paul Merker's story has recently been well told in Jeffrey Herf's *Divided Memory: The Nazi Past in the Two Germanys* (Cambridge, Mass.: Harvard University Press, 1997), although he does not mention the Klemperer incident.

135. See, for instance, his comment that "National Socialism has now become completely or almost completely identical with Bolshevism" (*I Shall Bear Witness,* p. 58, entry for March 19, 1934).

136. Ibid., p. 43, entry for December 31, 1933.

137. Ibid., p. 178, entry for August 29, 1936.

138. Ibid., p. 369, entry for May 21, 1941.

139. *Ich will Zeugnis ablegen,* vol. 2, p. 636, entry for January 4, 1945.

140. Some observers have stressed Klemperer's opportunism: his conversion to Protestantism and his postwar edging toward the Jewish community when this was advantageous are emphasized in the hostile review by Eva Auf der Maur in *Freiburger Rundbrief. Zeitschrift für christlich-jüdische Begegnung* 6, no. 4 (1999): 297–300. See especially p. 298. One could add Klemperer's taking of the Nazi loyalty oath in 1933 and his postwar joining of the Communist Party as further evidence of such opportunism. This constituted, no doubt, a part of the man's make-up; but Klemperer cannot be reduced to that alone and thereby

simply dismissed. It is precisely in the complexity and manifold layers of his person, including these human weaknesses, and in his being caught up in such horrible circumstances that the fascination and depth lie.

141. See *So sitze ich denn zwischen allen Stühlen,* vol. 1, pp. 59–60.

142. Ibid., p. 57, entry for July 26, 1945.

143. Ibid., p. 146.

144. Clive James, in the symposium "International Books of the Year—and the Millennium," *Times Literary Supplement,* December 3, 1999, p. 12. Klemperer died in 1960. See my article "Comrade Klemperer: Communism, Liberalism and Jewishness in the DDR," *Journal of Contemporary History* (April 2001).

145. *Ich will Zeugnis ablegen,* vol. 2, p. 75, entry for April 28, 1942.

146. Ibid., pp. 83–84, entry for May 11, 1942.

147. *I Shall Bear Witness,* p. 279, entry for January 10, 1939.

148. *Curriculum Vitae,* vol. 1, p. 576.

149. Ibid., p. 105, entry for May 30, 1942.

150. *So sitze ich denn zwischen allen Stühlen,* p. 226.

Index

Achad Ha-am (Asher Ginzburg), 30
Adorno, Theodor, 105n57
Alter, Robert, 10, 37, 101n2, 102nn12,18, 105n58, 109n106
Antichrist, 15
Arendt, Hannah: and Bildung, 15–16; and Blücher, 43–44, 63–64, 117–118nn89–95; correspondence, 1; on Enlightenment, 60; and Europe, 68–69; and friendship, 41–45, 57, 62; and German-Jewish intellectuals, 66–68, 119n108; on Germans and Jews, 41–45, 57–63; and Hebrew, 64; and Heidegger, 43–56, 111nn16–20, 113–114n46; and Jaspers, 43–44, 55–63; on Jewish identity, 41–69; and Klemperer, 1–7, 70–71, 76–77, 78–79, 83, 86, 95, 98; and natality, 53–54; on National Socialism, 32, 49–56, 60–61; and Scholem, 36, 43–44, 57, 60, 62, 65–69, 76–77, 79, 83, 98, 108–109nn101,102, 110–111nn12–14; and self-hood, 41–69; and the (German) Sonderweg, 51; and tradition, 66–69; and Yiddish, 64; and Zionism, 42, 58–59, 63, 64, 67–68
Auschwitz, 50–51, 57, 75

Barash, Jeffrey Andrew, 115n60
Baron, Lawrence, 109n2
Barres, Maurice, 86

Beddow, Michael, 11, 101n6
Bellow, Saul, 39
Benhabib, Seyla, 112n29, 117n90
Benjamin, Walter, 11, 13, 22, 25, 33, 35, 42, 64, 107n83, 109–110n4
Bergmann, Hugo, 104n40
Bergson, Henri, 85
Biale, David, 101n2
Bildung, 15–17, 78–79, 97–98
Blau-Weiss, 63
Blau-Weisse Brille, 26
Blücher, Heinrich, 43, 44, 47, 49, 53, 54, 63–64, 66, 101n5, 117–118nn89–95
Blumenfeld, Kurt, 10, 43, 51, 56, 58, 65, 68
Boerner, Peter, 100n6
Böhme, Jakob, 12
Bolkosky, Sidney, 122n41
Bramson, Leon, 114n47
Brecht, Bertolt, 42
Brenner, Michael, 18, 102n11, 104n39
Broch, Hermann, 2, 43, 44
Buber, Martin, 26, 101nn3,4; and Jewish renewal, 11; Klemperer and, 90, 127n115; Scholem relationship to, 12–13, 17, 30, 102n12, 107n83
Buchenwald, 75
Bund der Eiferer (Society of Zealots), 19

Carotenuto, Aldo, 109n3
Cohen, Hermann, 21, 25
Corbin, Henry, 24

Steven E. Aschheim holds the Vigevani
Chair in European Studies and teaches in
the Department of History at the Hebrew
University of Jerusalem. He is the author
of *Brothers and Strangers: The East European
Jew in German and German-Jewish Consciousness, 1800–1923; The Nietzsche Legacy
in Germany, 1890–1990;* and *Culture and Catastrophe: German and Jewish Confrontations
with National Socialism and Other Crises.* His
*In Times of Crisis: Essays on European Culture,
Germans and Jews,* will appear in 2001. He
is also the editor of the forthcoming con-
ference volume *Hannah Arendt in Jerusalem*
(2001).